a perfect love

Understanding John Wesley's
A Plain Account of Christian Perfection

Modern-Language Version and Notes by Steven W. Manskar
Theological Reflections by Marjorie Hewitt Suchocki
Study Guide by Diana L. Hynson

DISCIPLESHIP RESOURCES

PO BOX 340003 • NASHVILLE, TN 37203-0003
www.discipleshipresources.org

Cover and book design by Joey McNair

Edited by Linda R. Whited and Cindy S. Harris

ISBN 0-88177-426-X

Library of Congress Control Number 2004100287

DR426

Contents

Works of John Wesley Contained in *A Plain Account of Christian Perfection*

As you read *A Plain Account of Christian Perfection* you will notice that much of it is an anthology of works by John and Charles Wesley. From the sermon "Circumcision of the Heart," published in 1733, to the tract *Farther Thoughts on Christian Perfection*, published in 1763, these works span thirty years of John Wesley's ministry. Wesley included all this previously published material to support his argument that Christian perfection was always at the heart of Methodist preaching and ministry. He believed that this doctrine is what set the Methodists apart from other groups involved in the evangelical revival. This table is provided to help you see the breadth of Wesley's writings contained in *A Plain Account of Christian Perfection*.

Document Type	Document	Page #
Sermon 17	"The Circumcision of the Heart" (1733)	12–14
Hymns	*Hymns and Sacred Poems* (1739)	14–15
Tract	*The Character of a Methodist* (1741)	15–17
Sermon 40	"Christian Perfection" (1741)	18–21
Hymnal Preface	*Hymns and Sacred Poems* (1741)	23–25
Hymnal Preface	*Hymns and Sacred Poems* (1742)	27–28
Hymns	*Hymns and Sacred Poems* (1742)	28–30
Minutes	Conferences of 1744 and 1745	33–34
Minutes	Conferences of 1746 and 1747	34–37
Hymns	*Hymns and Sacred Poems* (1749)	37–39
Tract	*Thoughts On Christian Perfection* (1759)	41–52
Letter	From a friend (1762)	53–54
Letter to editor	Answering opponents (1762)	54–55
Memorial	The death of Jane Cooper (1761)	56–59
Tract	*Farther Thoughts on Christian Perfection* (1763)	61–86

John Wesley's "Operating Principles" of Theology and Ministry

Operating Principle #1
The Sovereign Love of God

- "'Love is the fulfilling of the law,' 'the end of the commandment.' It is not only 'the first and great' command, but all the commandments in one. 'Whatever is true, whatever is honorable, whatever is just, whatever is pure, whatever is pleasing, whatever is commendable, if there is any excellence and if there is anything worthy of praise,' they are all contained in this one word, *love*" (page 12).
- God's nature and name is love. This love is incarnate in Jesus Christ. The power of love liberates human beings and communities from the guilt and power of sin and death.
- Love heals and forms human character (holy tempers) into the character of Christ. "Love, the one perfect good, shall be your one ultimate goal. You shall desire one thing for its own sake—having the same mind that was in Christ Jesus, who is all in all" (page 12).

Operating Principle #2
The Reality of Sin and Sins

- *Sin* (that is, original sin, inbred sin) is alienation from God into which all human beings are born (Romans 5:12).
  - Sin damages the image of God.
  - Sin leads to sins.
- *Sins* are the transgressing of known laws of God.
- Wesley makes a crucial distinction between actual sins and human faults or mistakes.
  - Sins are voluntary transgressions of God's commandments (see page 43).
  - Mistakes that result from human ignorance or frailty are not considered by Wesley to be sins.
  - "...mistakes and any failings that necessarily flow from the corruptible state of the human body are not contrary to love. Therefore, according to Scriptural definition, they are not sin" (page 43).

Operating Principle #3
God's Love Is Revealed and Active in Grace: Prevenient, Justifying, and Sanctifying

- Prevenient grace awakens and prepares humans to accept God's acceptance in Jesus Christ.
- Justifying grace restores relationship through faith.
  - The guilt of sin is removed through forgiveness and repentance.
- Sanctifying grace liberates and forms character.
  - The power of sin is removed.
  - The image of Christ is healed.
  - Holy tempers are formed (Galatians 5:22-23).
  - Love is fully formed (Matthew 5:48).
  - Holiness of heart and life (Galatians 5:6)
  - Having the mind of Christ (Philippians 2:5)

Operating Principle #4
Connectionalism Is Essential for Going On to Perfection in Love

- Societies (local) (see page 78)
  - Classes and class leaders
  - Bands
  - Select societies
- Conference (regional) (see page 33)
  - Quarterly
  - Annual

Brief Chronology of John Wesley's Life

1703 Birth at Epworth, Lincolnshire

1709 Epworth rectory burns. John is rescued from his second-story room, "a brand plucked from the burning."

1714 Enters Charterhouse School, London.

1720 Enters Christ Church College, Oxford.

1725 Ordained deacon.

1726 Elected fellow of Lincoln College, Oxford.

1728 Ordained priest.

1729 Resident tutor at Lincoln College.

1730 Helps to organize and lead the Holy Club at Oxford.

1735 Samuel Wesley, Sr., dies.

Embarks on mission in Georgia.

1738 Returns to England. Meets Peter Böhler, a Moravian preacher.

Forms Fetter Lane Society with Moravians in London.

Experience of assurance of salvation at Aldersgate Street.

Visits Moravian community at Herrnhut in Germany.

1739 Begins field preaching around Bristol.

Samuel Wesley, Jr., dies.

1740 Breaks with the society at Fetter Lane and forms a new society at the Foundry.

The "New Room" is built in Bristol.

Lay speaking encouraged and supported.

1741 *The Character of a Methodist*

1742 Organizes first classes with the societies in Bristol.

Susanna Wesley dies.

1743 "The Appeals to Men of Reason and Religion"

"The Nature, Design, and General Rules of Our United Societies"

Wednesbury riot

1744 First Methodist Conference

1746 *Sermons on Several Occasions* published.

Establishes "credit union" for the poor and free medical clinic in London.

1747 *Primitive Physic: An Easy and Natural Method of Curing Most Diseases*

1751 Marries Mary Vazeille.

1756 *Notes Upon the New Testament* published

1759 *Thoughts on Christian Perfection*

1763 Women preachers

1765 "The Scripture Way of Salvation"

1767 *A Plain Account of Christian Perfection*

1768 "Free Thoughts on the Present State of Public Affairs"

Shortage of Methodist preachers for England, Ireland, and America

1769 Richard Boardman and Joseph Pilmore sent to serve the Methodists in America.

1770 George Whitefield dies.

1771 Francis Asbury sent to America.

1773 "Thoughts on the Present Scarcity of Provisions"

1774 "Thoughts Upon Slavery"

1775 "Calm Address to Our American Colonies"

1778 *Arminian Magazine* begins publication.

New chapel in City Road, London, opens.

1780 *A Collection of Hymns for the Use of The People Called Methodists*

1781 Mary Vazeille dies.

1784 "A Deed of Declaration" and ordinations

The Sunday Service of the Methodists in North America

1788 Charles Wesley dies.

1791 John Wesley dies at his home in London.

A Perfect Love: Understanding John Wesley's *A Plain Account of Christian Perfection*

Modern-Language Version and Notes by Steven W. Manskar

Contents

A Perfect Love: Understanding John Wesley's *A Plain Account of Christian Perfection*
Modern-Language Version and Notes by Steven W. Manskar

(Note: The Roman numeral divisions used in this book are intended to facilitate small-group study. Each Roman numeral represents a block of text that could be easily read and studied during a week. These are not found in Wesley's original work.)

Introduction

> [Jesus said,] "Be perfect, therefore, as your heavenly Father is perfect."
>
> (Matthew 5:48)

Christian perfection is one of the most distinctive doctrines of the Wesleyan tradition. John Wesley preached and taught and fought for it most of his life. *A Plain Account of Christian Perfection* is his reasoned defense of the doctrine that came to define his life and the evangelical movement that came to bear his name.

Christian perfection is the goal of all committed Methodists. Two of the historic questions asked of all men and women seeking ordination as United Methodist elders and deacons are, "Are you going on to perfection?" and, "Do you expect to be made perfect in love in this life?" (From *The Book of Discipline of The United Methodist Church—2000*. Copyright © 2000 by The United Methodist Publishing House. Used by permission; ¶ 327, page 214.)

The correct answer to both questions is yes. However, most ordinands today, along with most annual conference members, are uncomfortable with the questions and with the answer they are expected to give. They are uncomfortable because the questions sound arcane and naive. Christian perfection is rarely, if ever, preached from United Methodist pulpits or taught in seminary classrooms. It is seen by many as a historical and theological curiosity that is best left in the eighteenth century with Mr. Wesley.

This book is an effort to reclaim this important part of Methodist and Christian identity. The doctrine of Christian perfection is just as important today as it was in Wesley's day. This doctrine is at the heart of who Methodists are as a people and as a movement. All who claim the Wesleyan and Methodist heritage as their own need to study and understand Christian perfection, for in so doing they will seek it for themselves and for their church to the glory of God the Father, the Son, and the Holy Spirit.

One of the reasons the doctrine of Christian perfection is scoffed at and dismissed by so many is its name. When people hear the words *Christian* and *perfection* together, the word *impossible* immediately jumps to mind. This response is common because the meaning they hear in the

Thanks go to Dr. Marjorie Suchocki for the genesis of this project, and to Drs. Sarah Lancaster, Randy Maddox, and David Lowes Watson for reviewing the manuscript for theological and historical accuracy. Their contributions and support are deeply appreciated.

English word *perfection* is that of the Latin word *perfectio*. This term is the perfection of the gods. It means one who is perfect in all regards—in thought, word, and deed. Human beings are, of course, not capable of such perfection. But this is not the meaning of *Christian perfection*.

Wesley, and others who addressed the doctrine, took the meaning of *perfection* from the Greek words *teleios* and *teleiosis*. When these words appear in Scripture, the English word frequently used to convey their meaning is *perfect, perfection,* or *to be made perfect*. This interpretation is especially true with the King James Version of the Bible, which was the English Bible used by Wesley. He also read the Scriptures in the original languages, Hebrew and Greek.

Several English words are used today to convey the meaning of *teleios*: *whole, complete, mature, grown-up, perfect*. These words give us a more complete and accurate understanding of the meaning of *Christian perfection*. As you will learn as you read the following pages, Christian perfection is not *perfectio*, the perfection of the gods. Christian perfection is the work of divine grace that, through faith in Jesus Christ, restores the human soul, damaged by sin, to wholeness and helps babes in Christ to grow up to maturity in faith and love. Christian perfection is nothing more, or less, than growing up in love and becoming a whole, complete human being made in the image of God as revealed in Jesus Christ.

The best, most accurate description of Christian perfection is love. It is love fully formed in the human heart, soul, and mind. With Christian perfection the heart is so filled with love that there is no longer room for sin and evil to reside there. One who is perfected in love is consumed with loving God with heart, soul, mind, and strength and with loving neighbor as one's self. Love is the sole guiding principle and power of life. Christian perfection is letting "the same mind be in you that was in Christ Jesus" (Philippians 2:5, NRSV).

As you read this book, you will find that Wesley's argument for Christian perfection is firmly grounded in Scripture. He argues convincingly that this is not his doctrine, or the Methodists' doctrine. Perfection in love is biblical, and it is God's will for all of humankind and for the cosmos.

In order to make John Wesley's important book accessible to contemporary readers, we have edited his eighteenth-century English. Every effort has been made to preserve Wesley's original meaning. Some archaic terms have been replaced with modern alternatives. Word order and phrasing have been made more contemporary. Scripture references have been identified in endnotes located at the end of each section. Marginal notes have been added to explain some important terms and names. Some hymn stanzas from Charles Wesley's work have been included because the Wesley brothers worked in concert to help the people called Methodist to grow up in love, to go on to perfection in love.

Steven W. Manskar
Director, Accountable Discipleship
The General Board of Discipleship
Nashville, Tennessee

A Plain Account of Christian Perfection

1. In the following pages I intend to give a plain and clear account of the steps that led me, over the course of many years, to embrace the doctrine of Christian perfection. I owe this to those brothers and sisters who desire to know all "the truth as it is in Jesus."[1] Those deeply committed Christians are the ones concerned about questions of this kind. I will clearly declare the doctrine as it is, striving to show both what I thought from one period to another and why I thought so.

2. In the year 1725, when I was twenty-three years old, I read **Bishop Taylor**'s *Rule and Exercises of Holy Living and Dying*. In reading several parts of this book, I was deeply moved. I was particularly affected by the section dealing with purity of intention. I instantly resolved to dedicate all my thoughts, and words, and actions—all my life—to God. I was thoroughly convinced that there was no middle ground. Every part of my life, not only some of it, must be a sacrifice either to God or to myself, which is the same as to the devil.

Can any serious person doubt this or find a middle ground between serving God and serving the devil?

3. In the year 1726 I read **Thomas à Kempis**'s *The Imitation of Christ*. The nature and extent of inward religion, the religion of the heart, now appeared to me in a stronger light than it ever had before. I saw that giving all my life to God (supposing it is possible to do this without going further) would gain me nothing unless I gave my heart, indeed *all* my heart, to God.

I saw that "simplicity of intention, and purity of affection"—one intent in all we speak or do and one desire ruling all our **tempers**—are indeed "the wings of the soul," without which she can never ascend to the mount of God.

4. A year or two after that, **Mr. Law**'s *Christian Perfection* and *Serious Call* were put into my hands. These convinced me more than ever of the absolute impossibility of being half a Christian. I resolved through God's grace (the absolute necessity of which I was deeply aware) to be completely devoted to God, to give God all my soul, my body, and my possessions.

Will any considerate person say that this is carrying matters too far? Is anything less due to God, who has given Self for us, than to give God ourselves, all we have and all we are?

Bishop Taylor: Jeremy Taylor (1613–1667) was an Anglican bishop known particularly for his devotional writings that were expressions of Anglican spirituality. He encouraged a disciplined life that emphasized balance between piety and mercy. The work cited here is his most well known.

Thomas à Kempis: a fifteenth-century German priest known for his writings on Christian piety. One of his best known and influential works is *The Imitation of Christ*. He was important in Wesley's Christian formation and to his developing understanding of Christian perfection.

tempers: attitudes, temperament, and disposition. Wesley is concerned with the formation of holy tempers in the lives of Christians. They are synonymous with the fruit of the Spirit named by Paul in Galatians 5:22-23. These holy tempers are the building blocks of Christian character.

William Law: an eighteenth-century English theologian and teacher best known for his books *Christian Perfection* and *Serious Call to a Devout and Holy Life*. He was important in Wesley's Christian formation and to his developing understanding of Christian perfection.

5. In the year 1729 I began not only to read but to study the Bible as the only standard of truth and model of pure religion. For that reason I saw in a clearer and clearer light the fundamental need of having "the mind which was in Christ"[2] and of "walking as Christ also walked."[3] My study of Scripture helped me realize that Christians are to seek not just a part of but all of the mind of Christ. We are to strive to walk as he walked not just in some respects but in all things. This was the light that helped me see Christianity to be a consistent following of Christ. It is a complete inward and outward conformity to our Master. The only thing I feared was allowing my own experience, or the experience of others, to distort the message of the Bible to suit my own goals or desires. I could no longer live apart from the pattern of life given to the world in Jesus Christ.

6. On January 1, 1733, I preached on "The Circumcision of the Heart" before the University [Oxford] in St. Mary's church. The message is summarized in these lines:

> It is that habitual character of the soul that is known in Scripture as holiness. It directly implies being cleansed from sin, "from all filthiness both of flesh and spirit."[4] Consequently, holiness is being gifted with those virtues that were in Christ Jesus. It is having our minds so renewed[5] as to be "perfect as our Father in heaven is perfect."[6]

In the same sermon I observed,

> "Love is the fulfilling of the law,"[7] "the end of the commandment."[8] It is not only "the first and great"[9] command, but all the commandments in one. "Whatever is true, whatever is honorable, whatever is just, whatever is pure, whatever is pleasing, whatever is commendable, if there is any excellence and if there is anything worthy of praise,"[10] they are all contained in this one word, *love*.
>
> In this is perfection, and glory, and happiness. The royal law of heaven and earth is: "You shall love the Lord your God with all your heart, and with all your soul, and with all your mind, and with all your strength."[11] Love, the one perfect good, shall be your one ultimate goal. You shall desire one thing for its own sake—having the same mind that was in Christ Jesus,[12] who is all in all. The singular happiness you shall propose to your souls is to have "fellowship with the Father and the Son,"[13] being "joined to the Lord in one spirit."[14]
>
> The goal you are to pursue to the end of time is the enjoyment of God in time and in eternity. Desire other things only if they help you attain this end. Love the creature—as it leads to the Creator. Let love be the end of every word and action. Let every affection, thought, word, and action be dependent upon this love. Whatever you desire or fear, whatever you seek or shun, whatever you think, speak, or do, may it be in accord with your happiness in God, which is the sole end, as well as source, of your being.

John and Charles Wesley worked closely together. John was the preacher; Charles the poet. John spoke to the head; Charles to the heart. In boxes like this one throughout this work are selected hymns by Charles Wesley on the doctrine of Christian perfection. We invite you to meditate on them, to pray with them, and to sing them. We offer them as a way to help you understand and appreciate the Scripture way of salvation known as Christian perfection.

That blessed law of thine,
Jesu, to me impart;
Thy Spirit's law of life divine,
O write it in my heart!
Implant it deep within,
Whence it may ne'er remove,
The law of liberty from sin,
The perfect law of love.

Collection, #331, stanza 2

I concluded with these words:

> Here is the sum of the perfect law, the circumcision of the heart. Let the spirit return to God that gave it, with all that it holds dear. God does not ask of us any sacrifices other than the living sacrifice of the heart. Let our hearts be constantly offered up to God through Christ in flames of holy love.
>
> Let no human being hold your ultimate loyalty or devotion, for the Lord is a jealous God. God will not share the Lord's throne with another. In other words, God must reign without rival. Let there be no thought or desire of the heart that does not have the love of God as its ultimate objective. This is the way those saints of God, who still speak to us, once walked: "Yearn to live only in the way that is praise to God's name. Let all your thoughts, words, and works lead to God's glory." "Let your soul be filled with so complete a love of God that you may love nothing but for God's sake." "Have a pure intention of heart and steadfast regard for God's glory in all your actions." This is apparent when in every motion of our heart, every word of our tongue, every work of our hands we "pursue nothing that isn't in relation to God and in service to God's will." When we also neither think, nor speak, nor act to fulfill "our own will, but the will of God who sent us,"[15] when "whether we eat or drink, or whatever we do," we do it all "to the glory of God,"[16] then, and only then, is that "mind in us that was also in Christ Jesus."[17]

This sermon was the first of all my writings to be published. It contained the description of faith I had then, which then I chose not to call perfection. Without any material addition or subtraction, this is the view I have of it today. What is here that any person of understanding, who believes the Bible, can object to? Without flatly contradicting the Scripture, what can one deny? What may be removed without taking from the Word of God?

7. My brother and I remained in agreement upon this view of Christian faith (with all those young gentlemen called Methodists in derision) until we embarked for America near the end of 1735. It was the next year, while I was at Savannah, Georgia, that I wrote the following lines:

> Is there a thing beneath the sun,
>   That strives with thee my heart to share?
> Ah! tear it thence, and reign alone
>   The Lord of every motion there!

In the beginning of the year 1738, as I was returning from Georgia, the cry of my heart was,

> O grant that nothing in my soul
>   May dwell, but thy pure love alone!
> O may thy love possess me whole,

God of eternal truth and grace,
    Thy faithful promise seal!
Thy word, thy oath to Abraham's race,
    In us, even us fulfil.

Let us, to perfect love restored,
    Thy image here receive;
And in the presence of our Lord
    The life of angels live.

That mighty faith on me bestow
    Which cannot ask in vain,
Which holds, and will not let thee go
    Till I my suit obtain.

Till thou into my soul inspire
    The perfect love unknown,
And tell my infinite desire,
    Whate'er thou wilt, be done.

But is it possible that I
    Should live, and sin no more?
Lord, if on thee I dare rely,
    The faith shall bring the power.

On me that faith divine bestow
    Which doth the mountain move;
And all my spotless life shall show
    Th'omnipotence of love.

Collection, #333

My joy, my treasure, and my crown!
Strange fires far from my heart remove;
My every act, word, thought, be love!

I never heard that anyone objected to this. Indeed, who can object? Isn't this the language not only of every believer but of every one that is truly awakened? What have I written, to this day, that is either stronger or clearer?

Arvid Gradin: a member of the Moravian community at Herrnhut. Wesley regarded him as an example of one who had been cleansed from all sin.

8. In the following August, I had a long conversation with **Arvid Gradin** in Germany. After he had given me an account of his experience, I asked him to give me, in writing, a definition of "the full assurance of faith."[18] The following is what he wrote:

Rest in the blood of Christ; a firm confidence in God and persuasion of God's favor; the highest tranquility, serenity, and peace of mind, with a deliverance from every fleshly desire, and a cessation of all, even inward, sins.

This was the first account I ever heard from any living man of what I had previously learned from the Bible and had been praying for (with the small group of my friends) and expecting for several years.

9. In 1739 my brother and I published a volume of *Hymns and Sacred Poems*. In many of these we declared our sentiments strongly and explicitly.

Turn the full stream of nature's tide;
    Let all our actions tend
To thee, their source; thy love the guide,
    Thy glory be the end.

Earth then a scale to heaven shall be;
    Sense shall point out the road;
The creatures all shall lead to thee,
    And all we taste be God.

Again—

Lord, arm me with thy Spirit's might,
    Since I am call'd by thy great name:
In thee my wand'ring thoughts unite,
    Of all my works be thou the aim:
Thy love attend me all my days,
And my sole business be thy praise.

Again—

Eager for thee I ask and pant,
    So strong the principle divine,
Carries me out with sweet constraint,
    Till all my hallow'd soul be thine;
Plunged in the Godhead's deepest sea,
And lost in thine immensity!

14

Once more—

> Heavenly Adam, life divine,
> Change my nature into thine;
> Move and spread throughout my soul,
> Actuate and fill the whole.

It would be easy to cite many more passages to the same effect. These are enough to show, beyond contradiction, what our beliefs were at that time.

10. The first tract I ever wrote specifically on this subject was published near the end of this year. So that no one may be biased before they read it, I gave it the ordinary title *The Character of a Methodist*. In it I described a perfect Christian, placing at the beginning, "Not as though I had already attained."[19] Part of it I offer here without any change:

> A Methodist is one who loves the Lord God with all the heart, with all the soul, with all the mind, and with all the strength. God is the joy of a Methodist's heart, and the desire of his or her soul, which is continually crying, "Whom have I in heaven but you? And there is nothing on earth that I desire other than you."[20] My God and my all! You are "the strength of my heart and my portion forever."[21] A Methodist is, therefore, happy in God—indeed always happy, as if there were a well of water springing up to everlasting life filling the soul to overflowing with peace and joy.
>
> Perfect love having now cast out fear,[22] a Methodist is always rejoicing. In fact, the joy is so full that all a Methodist's bones cry out, "Blessed be the God and Father of our Lord Jesus Christ! By his great mercy he has given us a new birth . . . from the dead, and into an inheritance that is imperishable, undefiled, and unfading, kept in heaven" for me.[23]
>
> A Methodist who has this hope is so full of eternal life that he or she gives thanks in everything, knowing that this (whatever it is) is the will of God in Christ Jesus. Methodists cheerfully receive everything from Christ, saying, "The Lord's will is good";[24] and whether God gives or takes away, a Methodist equally blesses the Lord's name. In ease or pain, in sickness or health, in life or death, Methodists give thanks from the bottom of their hearts to God, who orders everything for good. They have wholly committed body and soul "into the hands of a faithful Creator."[25] They have "cast all care on God who cares for them." Because of this they fear nothing and "in all things" rest on Christ, having made their "request known to God with thanksgiving."[26]
>
> For indeed Methodists "pray without ceasing."[27] The constant prayer of the heart is this: "To you, O God, is my mouth, though without a voice. My silence speaks to you, my God." At all times and in all places a Methodist's heart is lifted up to God, never hindered, much less interrupted, by any person or thing. In seclusion or with others, in leisure,

O for a heart to praise my God,
 A heart from sin set free!
A heart that always feels thy blood,
 So freely spilt for me!

A heart resigned, submissive, meek,
 My great Redeemer's throne,
Where only Christ is heard to speak,
 Where Jesus reigns alone.

O for a lowly, contrite heart,
 Believing, true, and clean,
Which neither life nor death can part
 From him that dwells within!

A heart in every thought renewed,
 And full of love divine,
Perfect, and right, and pure, and good—
 A copy, Lord, of thine!

Thy tender heart is still the same,
 And melts at human woe;
Jesus, for thee distressed I am—
 I want thy love to know.

My heart, thou know'st, can never rest
 Till thou create my peace,
Till, of my Eden repossessed,
 From every sin I cease.

Fruit of thy gracious lips, on me
 Bestow that peace unknown,
The hidden manna, and the tree
 Of life, and the white stone.

Thy nature, gracious Lord, impart;
 Come quickly from above;
Write thy new name upon my heart,
 Thy new, best name of love!

Collection, #334

business, or conversation, a Methodist's heart is always with the Lord. When going to bed at night and when rising in the morning, "God is in all thoughts." Methodists walk with God continually. The loving eye of the soul is set on Christ and "seeing God who is invisible"[28] everywhere.

Methodists love God and love others as self.[29] They love every person as their own soul. They love enemies, even the enemies of God. If it is not in a Methodist's power to "do good to those who hate," he or she does not stop praying for those who hate, even though they reject love and continue to abuse and persecute.[30]

For a Methodist is "pure in heart."[31] Love has purified the heart from envy, bitterness, resentment, and every unkind temper. Love has cleansed the Methodist from pride, from which comes only strife.[32] Methodists have put on "compassion, kindness, humility, meekness, and patience."[33] Indeed, the Methodist has removed all possible ground for strife on his or her part. Because a Methodist does not love the world, nor any of the things of the world, no one can take what he or she desires. All desire is for God and for living as one who bears God's name.

Accordingly, this one desire is the one purpose of a Methodist's life: "To do, not his or her own will, but the will of God."[34] A Methodist's one ambition, at all times and in all places, is not to please self but to please the One whom his or her soul loves. A Methodist has a healthy eye. Because the "eye is healthy, the whole body is full of light. The whole is light, as when the bright shining of a candle enlightens the house."[35] God reigns alone. All that is in the soul is "holiness to the Lord." There is not a motion in a Methodist's heart that is not in accordance with God's will. Every thought that arises points to God and is in obedience to the law of Christ.[36]

"The tree is known by its fruits."[37] Because Methodists love God, they keep God's commandments—not just some of them or most of them, but all of them, from the least to the greatest. They are not satisfied to "keep the whole law and fail in one point,"[38] but have in all points "a clear conscience toward God and all people."[39] Methodists avoid whatever God has forbidden and do whatever God has commanded. A Methodist lives by God's commandments;[40] now God has set the heart free. It is God's glory and joy to do this. It is the Methodist's joy every day to "do the will of God on earth, as it is done in heaven."[41]

Because of love for God with the whole heart, Methodists strive to keep all of God's commandments with all their might. Love is the source of this obedience. Therefore, loving God with the whole heart, Methodists serve God with all their strength. A Methodist constantly presents his or her soul and "body as a living sacrifice, holy, acceptable to God."[42] Without reserve Methodists completely devote themselves, all they have and are, to the glory of God. Every power and strength of the Methodist's soul, every part of his or her body, and all of his or her talents are constantly employed according to the Master's will.

> The word of God is sure,
>   And never can remove;
> We shall in heart be pure,
>   And perfected in love;
> Rejoice in hope, rejoice with me,
> We shall from all our sins be free.
>
> Then let us gladly bring
>   Our sacrifice of praise;
> Let us give thanks, and sing,
>   And glory in his grace;
> Rejoice in hope, rejoice with me,
> We shall from all our sins be free.
>
> *Collection*, #336, stanzas 7–8

Consequently, "whatever a Methodist does, it is all to the glory of God."[43] Methodists not only *aim at* this in all efforts, which is implied in having a healthy eye, but actually *attain* it. Work and leisure, as well as prayers, all serve to this great end. Whether "sitting in the house, or walking by the way,"[44] whether lying down or rising up, Methodists promote, in all words and actions, the one business of life. Whether getting dressed, or working, or eating and drinking, or playing, everything tends to advance the glory of God through peace and good will among people. One invariable rule is this: "Whatever you do, in word or deed, do everything in the name of the Lord Jesus, giving thanks to God the Father through him."[45]

The customs of the world do not hinder a Methodist's "running the race that is set before him or her."[46] Methodists cannot therefore "store up . . . treasures on earth,"[47] any more than they can take fire into their bosoms. Methodists cannot speak evil of a neighbor any more than they can lie either for God or human being. Methodists cannot speak an unkind word of anyone, for love keeps the door of the lips. Methodists cannot speak idle words.[48] "No corrupt conversation" ever "comes out of a Methodist's mouth."[49] Everything that is not "useful for building up" is not fit to "give grace to those who hear."[50] Methodists think, speak, and act according to "whatever is pure, whatever is pleasing, whatever is commendable"[51] in such a way that all life is "adorning the doctrine of God our Savior in all things."[52]

These are the very words in which I, for the first time, described in detail my beliefs regarding Christian perfection. This became the focus of my ministry in the year 1725. It became all the more important in 1730, when I began to be **_homo unius libri_**, "a man of one book." This means that I began to regard the Bible as the primary source for doctrine and ministry.

This is the very same doctrine that I believe and teach today. I have not added one point to either that inward or that outward holiness that I affirmed thirty-eight years ago. By the grace of God, it is the same that I have continued to teach for all these years. This will become apparent to every impartial person who reads the following extracts.

11. To this day, and for some time, I do not know that any writer has made any objection against *The Character of a Methodist.* I did not find much opposition at the beginning, at least not from serious people. But after a time a cry arose that surprised me because it came from among religious people. They did not object to my description of perfection. Rather, they insisted that there is no perfection on earth and vehemently attacked my brother and me for affirming the contrary. We did not expect so rough an attack from fellow brothers in Christ. This attack was surprising to us because we were clear that justification is by faith and all of salvation is a gift by the simple grace of God. But what surprised us most was that we were said to dishonor Christ by

homo unius libri: Wesley did not mean that his reading was limited to only the Bible. Instead he meant that Scripture is the sole measure of Christian belief and practice. Wesley was a voracious reader and encouraged the Methodist preachers to follow his example of diligent study of human knowledge about God and God's world.

> Reign in me, Lord, thy foes control
>   Who would not own thy sway;
> Diffuse thine image through my soul,
>   Shine to the perfect day.
>
> Scatter the last remains of sin,
>   And seal me thine abode;
> O make me glorious all within,
>   A temple built by God!
>
> *Collection*, #338, stanzas 4–5

asserting that he "saves to the uttermost,"[53] by maintaining that he alone will reign in our hearts and "make all things subject to himself."[54]

12. I think it was toward the end of 1740 that I had a conversation with Dr. Gibson, then Bishop of London, at Whitehall. He asked me what I meant by perfection. I told him without any pretense or reserve. When I stopped speaking, he said, "Mr. Wesley, if this is all you mean, publish it to all the world. If anyone then can refute what you say, he may have free leave." I answered, "My Lord, I will," and accordingly wrote and published the sermon on Christian perfection (1741). In that sermon I intended to reveal (1) in what sense Christians are not perfect, and (2) in what sense they are perfect.

(1) In what sense Christians are not perfect: They are not perfect in knowledge. They are not free from ignorance or from making mistakes. We cannot expect anyone to be infallible or omniscient. Christians are not free from frailties such as slowness of understanding, impulsiveness or solemnity, impropriety of language, and inarticulate pronunciation. One might add to this a thousand nameless defects, either in conversation or behavior. None are perfectly freed from shortcomings such as these until their spirits return to God. Because "the servant is not above his master,"[55] we cannot expect to be entirely freed from temptation until the end of this life. There cannot be, in this sense, any absolute perfection on earth. There is no perfection of parts or characteristics of a person. Rather, it is a process of growth and maturity of the whole person.

(2) In what sense, then, are they perfect? Look, we are not speaking of babes in Christ but of adult Christians. But even babes in Christ are so far perfect as not to commit <u>sin</u>.[56] Saint John explicitly affirms this. This is not contradicted by examples of the Old Testament. If the holiest of the ancient Jews did sometimes commit sin, we cannot conclude from them that all Christians do and must commit sin as long as they live.

But doesn't the Scripture say, "A just man sins seven times a day?" It does not. Indeed, it says, "A just man falls seven times."[57] But this is beside the point. First, the words *a day* are not in the text. Secondly, here is no mention of falling into sin at all. What is mentioned here is falling into worldly hardship.

But elsewhere Solomon says, "There is no man who does not sin."[58] Certainly it was so in the days of Solomon. Indeed, from Solomon to Christ there was no one that did not sin. But whatever was the case of those under the law, we may safely affirm, with Saint John, that since the gospel was given, "those who are born of God do not sin."[59]

<u>The privileges of Christians</u> are not to be limited by what the Old Testament says concerning the people of God (such as Noah, Abraham, Sarah, Jacob, Esau, Joseph, Moses, Miriam, David, and so forth) before the advent of Christ. We see now that the fullness of time has come, the Holy Spirit has been given, the great salvation of God is now brought to all people

sin: Wesley understands sin to be transgression of known laws. Sins are willful disobedience of God, and violations of God's commands. Christians are people who have been restored to right relationship with God (justification), whose character is being conformed to "having the mind of Christ" (Philippians 2:5), and who are "working out their own salvation" (Philippians 2:12-13) (sanctification). By virtue of the relational (justification) and real (sanctification) changes God has made—and is making—in them, Christians do not willfully transgress known laws of God. Therefore, Wesley can rightly say that Christians do not sin (1 John 3:9).

the privileges of Christians: include the life of holiness given to all by grace and faith in Christ. This privilege is to love God with our whole selves and to love our neighbor as ourselves. The privilege of Christians is life lived with God through Christ. It is new birth and sanctification, along with the gifts and fruit of the Spirit (1 Corinthians 12:4-11; Galatians 5:22-26).

18

by the revelation of Jesus Christ. The kingdom of heaven is set up on earth now. The Spirit of God declared in Old Testament times concerning this, "The feeblest among them on that day shall be like David, and the house of David shall be like God, like the angel of the LORD, at their head."[60] (David is far from being the pattern or standard of Christian perfection.)

But the apostles themselves committed sin. For example, Peter denied Christ, and Paul engaged in harsh conflict with Barnabas. Supposing they did, will you then argue: "If two of the apostles committed sin, then all other Christians, in all ages, do and must commit sin as long as they live"? No! God forbid we should speak in this way. The inevitability of sin was not imposed upon them. The grace of God was certainly sufficient for them, just as it is sufficient for us today.

But Saint James says, "For all of us make many mistakes."[61] This is true. About whom is Saint James speaking? He is not speaking of the apostle himself, nor any real Christian. Rather, he is speaking of those many teachers whom God has not sent. This is a figure of speech that cannot be applied to either the apostle or any true believer. Evidence of this is found in James 3:9, "With it we bless the Lord and Father, and with it we curse those who are made in the likeness of God" (NRSV). Certainly not the apostle or we believers! Secondly, from James 3:1-2, "Not many of you should become teachers, my brothers and sisters, for you know that we who teach will be judged with greater strictness. For all of us make many mistakes" (NRSV). *We!* Who? Not the apostles nor true believers but those who were to "be judged with greater strictness" because of those many mistakes. No, thirdly, the verse itself proves that the phrase "all of us make many mistakes" cannot be spoken either of all people or of all Christians. This is so because the verse goes on to contrast the "all of us" with the one who "makes no mistakes" and is declared "perfect."[62]

But Saint John himself says, "If we say that we have no sin, we deceive ourselves,"[63] and, "If we say we have not sinned, we make him [God] a liar, and his word is not in us."[64]

I answer, (1) 1 John 1:10 establishes the meaning of verse 8. "If we say that we have no sin" in verse eight is explained by "If we say we have not sinned" in verse ten. (2) The point under consideration is not whether we have or have not sinned up to now. Neither of these verses asserts that we do sin, or commit sin now. (3) The ninth verse explains both the eighth and tenth: "If we confess our sins, he who is faithful and just will forgive us our sins and cleanse us from all unrighteousness" (NRSV). It is as if he had said, "I have affirmed before, the blood of Christ cleanses from all sin." No one can say, "I do not need it. I have no sin from which to be cleansed." "If we say that we have no sin" or that "we have not sinned," we deceive ourselves and make God a liar. But "if we confess our sins, he who is faithful and just" will not only "forgive us our sins" but also "cleanse us from all unrighteousness," that we may "go and sin no more."[65] Therefore, in conformity to both the doctrine of Saint John and the whole meaning of the New

Holy Lamb, who thee receive,
Who in thee begin to live,
Day and night they cry to thee,
As thou art, so let us be!

Jesu, see my panting breast!
See I pant in thee to rest!
Gladly would I now be clean;
Cleanse me now from every sin.

Fix, O fix my wavering mind,
To thy cross my spirit bind;
Earthly passions far remove;
Swallow up my soul in love.

Collection, #340, stanzas 1–3

Testament, we establish this conclusion: A Christian is perfect and does not commit sin.

This is the glorious privilege of every Christian, indeed, even if he is a mere babe in Christ. But it can be affirmed only of mature Christians that they are in such a sense perfect as to be freed from evil thoughts and evil tempers.

Consider first what it means to be set free from evil or sinful thoughts. Indeed, where do they come from? "For it is from within, from the human heart, that evil intentions come."[66] If, therefore, the heart is no longer evil, then evil thoughts no longer proceed from it, for "a good tree cannot bring forth evil fruit."[67]

Mature Christians are freed from evil tempers in the same way they are set free from evil thoughts. Every one of them can say with Saint Paul, "I have been crucified with Christ; and it is no longer I who live, but it is Christ who lives in me."[68] These words clearly describe a deliverance from inward sin as well as outward sin. This is expressed negatively: "It is no longer I who live." My evil nature, the body of sin, is destroyed. It is also expressed positively: "It is Christ," and therefore all that is holy and just and good, "who lives in me." Indeed, that "it is Christ who lives in me" and that "it is no longer I who live" are inseparably connected. For "what communion has light with darkness," or "Christ with Satan?"[69]

He, therefore, who lives in these Christians has "purified their hearts by faith,"[70] since every one who has Christ, "the hope of glory," purifies himself or herself "even as he [Christ] is pure."[71] Because Christ was lowly in heart, he is purified from pride. Because Christ desired to do only the will of his Father, he is pure from desire and self-will. And because Christ was meek and gentle, he is pure from anger in the common sense of the word. I say "in the common sense of the word" because he does have anger toward sin while he is grieved for the sinner. He feels repulsed at every offense against God, but feels only tender compassion for the offender.

In this way Jesus saves people from their sins. He saves them not only from outward sins but from the sins of their hearts. "True," say some, "but not until death and not in this world." On the contrary, Saint John says, "Love has been perfected among us in this: that we may have boldness on the day of judgment, because as he is, so are we in this world."[72] Beyond all contradiction, the apostle is speaking about himself and other living Christians, whom he clearly affirms are "like their Master" not only at or after death but "in this world."

His words in the first chapter correspond to this: "God is light, and in him there is no darkness at all. . . . If we walk in the light, as he is in the light, we have fellowship with one another, and the blood of Jesus Christ his Son cleanses us from all sin."[73] Also: "If we confess our sins, he who is faithful and just will forgive us our sins and cleanse us from all unrighteousness."[74] Now, it is clear that John is speaking of a salvation made complete in this world. For he does not say

> Come, Holy Ghost, all-quick'ning fire,
> Come, and my hallowed heart inspire,
>   Sprinkled with the atoning blood;
> Now to my soul thyself reveal,
> Thy mighty working let me feel,
>   And know that I am born of God.
>
> Thy witness with my spirit bear
> That God, my God, inhabits there,
>   Thou with the Father and the Son
> Eternal light's coeval beam;
> Be Christ in me, and I in him,
>   Till perfect we are made in one.
>
> *Collection, #341, stanza 1*

> When wilt thou my whole heart subdue?
> Come, Lord, and form my soul anew,
>   Emptied of pride, and wrath, and hell;
> Less than the least of all thy store
> Of mercies, I myself abhor;
>   All, all my vileness may I feel.
>
> Humble, and teachable, and mild,
> O may I, as a little child,
>   My lowly Master's steps pursue!
> Be anger to my soul unknown;
> Hate, envy, jealousy, be gone!
>   In love create thou all things new.
>
> *Collection, #341, stanza 2*

that the blood of Christ *will* cleanse (meaning at the hour of death, or in the day of judgment) but that it *cleanses* us living Christians "from all sin" now. It is equally apparent that if *any* sin remains, we are not cleansed from *all* sin. If *any* unrighteousness remains in the soul, it is not cleansed from *all* unrighteousness.

Do not let anyone say that this relates only to justification or to cleansing us from the guilt of sin. First, this would join together what the apostle clearly separates by saying first "will forgive us our sins" and then "and cleanse us from all unrighteousness." Secondly, this affirms justification by works in the strongest way possible because it requires all inward and outward holiness to precede justification. For if the cleansing mentioned here is no different from cleansing us from the guilt of sin, then we are not cleansed from guilt—not justified—unless we first walk "in the light as he himself is in the light."

The truth remains, however, that Christians are saved in this world from all sin, from all unrighteousness. They are now perfect in such a sense as to not commit sin and to be freed from evil thoughts and evil tempers.

I expected that ideas such as these would cause offense. After all, they directly contradict the beliefs of many of even the best Christians. For if these things are true, those people are not Christians at all. Therefore, I expected much hostile criticism. But, happily, I was disappointed. I do not know that any appeared, so I went quietly on my way.

> Let earth no more my heart divide;
> With Christ may I be crucified,
>   To thee with my whole soul aspire;
> Dead to the world and all its toys,
> Its idle pomp, and fading joys,
>   Be thou alone my one desire.
>
> Be thou my joy; be thou my dread;
> In battle cover thou my head,
>   Nor earth nor hell I then shall fear;
> I then shall turn my steady face;
> Want, pain defy, enjoy disgrace,
>   Glory in dissolution near.
>
> My will be swallowed up in thee;
> Light in thy light still may I see,
>   Beholding thee with open face:
> Called the full power of faith to prove,
> Let all my hallowed heart be love,
> And all my spotless life be praise.
>
> Come, Holy Ghost, all-quick'ning fire,
> My consecrated heart inspire,
>   Sprinkled with the atoning blood;
> Still to my soul thyself reveal,
> Thy mighty working may I feel,
>   And know that I am one with God!
>
> *Collection*, #341, stanzas 3–4

Endnotes

1. Ephesians 4:21
2. Philippians 2:5
3. 1 John 2:6
4. 2 Corinthians 7:1
5. See Ephesians 4:23.
6. Matthew 5:48
7. Romans 13:10
8. 1 Timothy 1:5
9. Matthew 22:38
10. Philippians 4:8, NRSV
11. Mark 12:30, NRSV
12. See Philippians 2:5.
13. 1 John 1:3
14. 1 Corinthians 6:17
15. John 5:30; 6:38
16. 1 Corinthians 10:31
17. Philippians 2:5
18. Hebrews 10:22
19. Philippians 3:12
20. Psalm 73:25, NRSV
21. Psalm 73:26
22. 1 John 4:18
23. 1 Peter 1:3-4, NRSV
24. 2 Kings 20:19; Isaiah 39:8
25. 1 Peter 4:19
26. Philippians 4:6
27. 1 Thessalonians 5:17, NRSV
28. Hebrews 11:27
29. Matthew 22:37-40
30. Matthew 5:44
31. Matthew 5:8
32. See Proverbs 13:10.
33. Colossians 3:12, NRSV
34. John 6:38
35. Matthew 6:22, 5:14-15
36. See Galatians 6:2.
37. Matthew 12:33
38. James 2:10
39. Acts 24:16, NRSV
40. Nehemiah 10:29
41. Matthew 6:10
42. Romans 12:1
43. 1 Corinthians 10:31
44. Deuteronomy 6:7
45. Colossians 3:17, NRSV
46. Hebrews 12:1
47. Matthew 6:19, NRSV
48. See Matthew 12:36.
49. Ephesians 4:29
50. Ephesians 4:29, NRSV
51. Philippians 4:8, NRSV
52. Titus 2:10
53. Hebrews 7:25
54. Philippians 3:21, NRSV
55. Matthew 10:24
56. See 1 John 3:9.
57. Proverbs 24:16
58. Ecclesiastes 7:20
59. 1 John 5:18, NRSV
60. Zechariah 12:8, NRSV
61. James 3:2, NRSV
62. James 3:1-2, NRSV
63. 1 John 1:8
64. 1 John 1:10
65. John 8:11
66. Mark 7:21, NRSV
67. Matthew 7:18
68. Galatians 2:19-20, NRSV
69. 2 Corinthians 6:14-15
70. Acts 15:9
71. 1 John 3:3
72. 1 John 4:17, NRSV
73. 1 John 1:5, 7
74. 1 John 1:9, NRSV

13. We published a second volume of hymns in the spring of 1741. Because the doctrine of Christian perfection was still misunderstood and, consequently, misrepresented, I set out to explain it more clearly. This was done in the hymnal's preface as follows:

> This great gift of God, the salvation of our souls, is nothing more or less than the image of God stamped afresh upon our hearts. It is a renewal of believers. The spirit of their mind is conformed to the mind of Christ. God has laid "the axe at the root of the tree, . . . purifying their hearts by faith."[1] <u>All the thoughts of their hearts have been cleansed by the inspiration of God's Holy Spirit.</u>
>
> Their hope is that they will see God as God is. It is in this hope that they purify themselves as God is pure. They strive to be holy, as God is holy. They live this out in the way they conduct themselves in the world. It is through the living out of this life, to which God has called them, that they grow and mature in faith and love. In this way they will someday become the people God created them to be. They live day to day, going "on from strength to strength,"[2] "seeing the glory of the Lord as though reflected in a mirror, . . . being transformed into the same image from one degree of glory to another" by "the Lord, the Spirit."[3]
>
> "Where the Spirit of the Lord is, there is freedom"[4] "from the law of sin and death."[5] Even though one such as I may tell them the good news, this freedom is too much to be believed by people who are blinded by the world. For Jesus has set those who are "born of God" free[6] from pride, that great root of sin and bitterness. They feel that all their "competence is from God."[7] God alone is in all their thoughts and "is at work in you, enabling you both to will and to work for his good pleasure."[8] They feel that when they speak, the Spirit of their Father speaks in them; and the work of their hands is guided by the hands of the Father who is in them.[9] God is everything to them. They are nothing in God's sight. They are freed from self-will. This means they desire nothing but the holy and perfect will of God. They do not seek comfort in poverty, ease in pain,[10] life, death, or any creature. Rather, they are continually crying in their inmost soul, "Father . . . , your will be done."[11]

"All the thoughts . . .": This is a reference to the "Collect for Purity" from the weekly eucharist liturgy of the *Book of Common Prayer*:

"Almighty God, unto whom all hearts are open, all desires known, and from whom no secrets are hid: Cleanse the thoughts of our hearts by the inspiration of thy Holy Spirit, that we may perfectly love thee, and worthily magnify thy holy Name; through Christ our Lord. Amen."

> Ever fainting with desire,
>   For thee, O Christ, I call!
> Thee I restlessly require,
>   I want my God, my All.
> Jesus, dear redeeming Lord,
> I want thy coming from above:
>   Help me, Saviour, speak the word,
>   And perfect me in love.
>
> *Collection*, #344, stanza 1

They are freed from evil thoughts, so that they cannot for a moment enter into them. Previously when an evil thought came in, they looked up and it vanished away. But now it does not come in, because there is no room for this in a soul that is full of God.

They are free from wanderings in prayer. When they urgently pour out their hearts before God, they think of nothing that is past, or absent, or to come.[12] Their thoughts are focused upon God alone. In times past, their thoughts wandered from one thing to another like smoke. But now that smoke does not rise at all.

They have no fear or doubt regarding either their general condition or any particular action.[13] The anointing from the Holy One[14] teaches them every hour what they shall do, and what they shall speak.[15] They trust in the Holy Spirit's teaching and obey, having no need to question it.[16]

They are in one sense freed from temptations. They are not troubled by the infinite temptations that fly about every day.[17] Their souls are even and calm at all times. Their hearts are faithful and unmovable. Their peace, flowing like a river, "surpasses all understanding,"[18] and they "rejoice with an indescribable and glorious joy."[19] For they "are sealed by the Spirit for the day of redemption,"[20] having the witness in themselves that "there is laid up for" them a "crown of righteousness, which the Lord will give" them "in that day."[21]

Now, this is not to condemn those who are not renewed in love as described above. On the contrary, whoever has a sure confidence in God and believes that their sins are forgiven through the work of Christ is a child of God. If God abides in them, they inherit all the promises of God. If their faith is weak or is being "tested with fire"[22] so that their souls "suffer various trials,"[23] they should not in any way discard their trust or deny the faith they have received.

We do not dare to affirm, as some have, that all this salvation is given at once. Indeed, there is both an instantaneous and a gradual work of God in God's children. We know there is no shortage of witnesses who have received, in an instant, either a clear sense of forgiveness of sins or the abiding witness of the Holy Spirit. But we do not know of a single instance, in any place, of someone receiving at the same time remission of sins, the abiding witness of the Spirit, and a new and clean heart.

Indeed, we cannot tell how God may work. But the general way in which God does work is this: The Spirit of God works on those who trust in their own **righteousness** and wealth, believing that they are self-sufficient. God's Word convinces them that they are poor and naked. Everything they have done is brought to their memory. It is laid before them so that they may see the wrath of God hanging over their heads. This helps them see that they deserve the damnation of hell. In their distress they cry out to the Lord. God shows them that their sins have been taken away, and God opens the kingdom of heaven in their hearts, "righteousness and peace and joy in the Holy Spirit."[24] Sorrow and pain flee

---

Wilt thou suffer me to go
Lamenting all my days?
Shall I never, never know
Thy sanctifying grace?
Wilt thou not the light afford,
The darkness from my soul remove?
Help me, Saviour, speak the word,
And perfect me in love.

Collection, #344, stanza 2

---

righteousness: right living or conduct according to the law, will, and Spirit of God. Because of original sin all human righteousness is suspect. No amount of good works will ever make a person righteous in God's eyes. Only Christ, through his work on the cross, attributes righteousness to humans. In other words, any righteousness attributed to humans actually belongs to Christ. However, as humans grow in holiness of heart and life, Christ's righteousness becomes more and more their own.

away and "sin has no more dominion over"[25] them. Knowing they are __justified__ freely through faith in his blood, they "have peace with God through Jesus Christ."[26] They "rejoice in hope of the glory of God,"[27] and "the love of God is poured into their hearts."[28]

They remain in this peace for days, or weeks, or months. They also commonly believe that they will no longer experience spiritual conflict, that is until they are assaulted again by some of their old enemies, the familiar sins, or the sin that most easily harasses them (such as anger or lust). Next comes fear and doubt. They fear that they will lose their faith. They doubt because they fear that God has forgotten them or because they fear that believing their sins were forgiven was nothing more than wishful thinking. Under these clouds they go mourning all the day long, especially if they negotiate with the devil. Soon after they reach this point of despair, the Lord answers. God sends the Holy Spirit to comfort them and to constantly remind them that they are children of God. They become meek and gentle and teachable. For the first time they see the source of their love. God would not reveal this to them before, because they were not ready to see or understand.

Now they see within themselves all the hidden corruption and the depths of pride, self-will, and hell. At the same time, they have the witness in themselves that even in the midst of this fiery trial,[29] "you are an heir of God and a joint heir with Christ."[30] This continually increases the strong sense they then have of their inability to help themselves and the inexpressible hunger they feel for a full renewal in Christ's image, in "true righteousness and holiness."[31] Then God is mindful of the longing of those who fear God. God gives them an honest and pure heart, stamps upon them God's own image and name, and creates them anew in Christ Jesus. God comes to them with the Son and the blessed Spirit and, dwelling in their souls, brings them into the "rest that remains for the people of God."[32]

I must remark here: (1) This is the strongest account we ever gave of Christian perfection. Indeed, it is too strong at some points, as indicated in some of the footnotes. (See footnotes 10, 12, 13, 15, 16, 17, 21.) (2) There is nothing on this subject that we have written since we wrote this, either in verse or prose, that is not contained either directly or indirectly in this preface. This is to attest that whether you believe our presentation of this doctrine to be right or wrong, it is the same as we have taught it from the beginning.

14. I do not need to give additional evidence of this by an abundance of quotations from the volume itself. It may suffice to cite part of one hymn, the last in that volume:

> Lord, I believe a rest remains,
> To all thy people known;
> A rest where pure enjoyment reigns,
> And thou art loved alone;

__justified:__ to be restored to right relationship with God. Wesley defined justification as forgiveness. It is a gift from God through Jesus Christ, crucified and risen.

> Lord, if I on thee believe,
> The second gift impart;
> With th'indwelling Spirit give
> A new, a contrite heart;
> If with love thy heart is stored,
> If now o'er me thy bowels move,
> Help me, Saviour, speak the word,
> And perfect me in love.
>
> *Collection,* #344, stanza 3

> Let me gain my calling's hope,
> O make the sinner clean!
> Dry corruption's fountain up,
> Cut off the' entail of sin;
> Take me into thee, my Lord,
> And I shall then no longer rove:
> Help me, Saviour, speak the word,
> And perfect me in love.
>
> *Collection,* #344, stanza 4

A rest where all our soul's desire
    Is fix'd on things above;
Where doubt and pain and fear expire,
    Cast out by perfect love.

From every evil motion freed,
    (The Son hath made us free,)
On all the powers of hell we tread,
    In glorious liberty.

Safe in the way of life, above
    Death, earth, and hell we rise;
We find, when perfected in love,
    Our long-sought paradise.

O that I now the rest might know,
    Believe, and enter in!
Now, Savior, now the power bestow,
    And let me cease from sin!

Remove this hardness from my heart,
    This unbelief remove:
To me the rest of faith impart,
    The sabbath of thy love.

Come, O my Savior, come away
    Into my soul descend!
No longer from thy creature stay,
    My author and my end.

The bliss thou hast for me prepared,
    No longer be delay'd:
Come, my exceeding great reward,
    For whom I first was made.

Come, Father, Son, and Holy Ghost,
    And seal me thine abode!
Let all I am in thee be lost:
    Let all be lost in God!

> Thou, my life, my treasure be,
>   My portion here below!
> Nothing would I seek but thee,
>   Thee only would I know,
>   My exceeding great reward,
> My heaven on earth, my heaven above:
> Help me, Saviour, speak the word,
>   And perfect me in love.
>
> *Collection*, #344, stanza 5

    Can anything be more clear than

(1) that this is as complete and exalted a salvation as we have ever taught?

(2) that this salvation is taught as being received by simple faith, and the only thing that can hinder it is unbelief?

(3) that this faith, and consequently the salvation it brings, is taught as being given in an instant?

(4) that it is supposed that instant may be now? that we need not wait another moment? that "now" is the very "now is the accepted time? now is the day of" this full "salvation"?[33]

(5) that if any teach otherwise, that person brings new doctrine among us?

15. We published another volume of hymns in the year 1742. With the dispute at its height, we spoke more clearly to the point than ever before. Accordingly, an abundance of the hymns in this volume specifically address this subject. The preface also speaks directly to the topic:

(1) Perhaps the general prejudice against Christian perfection may chiefly arise from a misunderstanding of its nature. We willingly allow and constantly declare that there is no perfection in this life that suggests either an exemption from doing good and attending all the **ordinances of God**, or freedom from ignorance, mistake, temptation, and a multitude of physical infirmities.

(2) First, we not only allow but earnestly contend that there is no perfection in this life that allows any immunity from practicing all the ordinances of God or from doing good to all people while we have time, "especially for those of the family of faith."[34] We believe that not only those who are newborn infants in Christ (who have recently found redemption in his blood), but also those who are grown up into perfect human beings[35] must, at every opportunity, eat bread and drink wine in remembrance of Christ and study the Scriptures. By fasting as well as moderation they are to "keep their bodies under, and bring them into subjection."[36] Above all, they are to pour out their souls in prayer, both secretly and in the great congregation.

(3) Secondly, we believe that there is no perfection in this life that suggests a complete deliverance either from ignorance or mistake in things not essential to salvation. Perfection in this life does not bring freedom from numerous temptations or countless physical ailments, by means of which the perishable body more or less oppresses the soul. We cannot find any evidence in Scripture that makes us think that any human being is wholly exempt either from bodily infirmities or from ignorance of many things. Nor can we find any evidence that makes us imagine anyone that is not vulnerable to mistake or falling into various temptations.

(4) But whom then do you mean by "one that is perfect?" We mean one in whom is "the mind that was in Christ,"[37] and who "walks as Christ walked."[38] We mean a man or woman "who has clean hands and a pure heart,"[39] or who is cleansed "from every defilement of body and of spirit,"[40] one in whom there is "no cause for stumbling"[41] and who, consequently, "does not sin."[42] To express this a little more precisely, we understand that scriptural expression "a perfect person"[43] to mean one in whom God has fulfilled God's faithful word: "You shall be clean from all your uncleannesses, and from all your idols I will cleanse you."[44] We understand by this, one whom God has "sanctified entirely in body, soul, and spirit,"[45] one who "walks in the light as God is in the light, in whom there is no

ordinances of God: the instituted means of grace; the basics of Christian discipleship that draw us to Christ and keep us with him. They include public worship of God, devotional reading and study, the Lord's Supper, family and private prayer, Bible study, and fasting or abstinence.

> Grant me now the bliss to feel
>   Of those that are in thee;
> Son of God, thyself reveal,
>   Engrave thy name on me;
> As in heaven be here adored,
> And let me now the promise prove:
> Help me, Saviour, speak the word,
>   And perfect me in love.
>
> *Collection*, #344, stanza 6

darkness at all, the blood of Jesus Christ, God's Son, having cleansed him from all sin."[46]

(5) This person can now testify to all humankind, "I have been crucified with Christ; and it is no longer I who live, but it is Christ who lives in me."[47] This person is "holy as God who called" him or her "is holy," both in heart and "in all conduct."[48] This person "loves the Lord God with all the heart"[49] and serves God "with all strength."[50] This person loves every person "as he or she loves self,"[51] indeed "as Christ loves us," and in particular this person loves those who "hate him and persecute him, because they do not know the Son or the Father."[52] Indeed this person's soul is all love, filled with "compassion, kindness, humility, meekness, and patience."[53] His or her life is guided by the soul, full of the "work of faith and labor of love and steadfastness of hope."[54] "And whatever" this person does, "in word or deed," he or she does "everything in the name," in the love and power, "of the Lord Jesus."[55] In a word, this person does "the will of God on earth, as it is done in heaven."[56]

(6) This is what it means to be a perfect human being: It means being "sanctified throughout;"[57] even "to have a heart so consumed with the love of God" (to use **Archbishop Usher**'s words) "as to constantly offer up every thought, word, and work as a spiritual sacrifice, acceptable to God through Christ."[58] In every thought of our hearts, in every word of our tongues, in every work of our hands, to "show forth God's praise, who has called us out of darkness into God's marvelous light."[59] O that both we and all who seek the Lord Jesus in sincerity may thus "be made perfect in one!"[60]

This is the doctrine that we preached from the beginning and that we preach today. Indeed, we looked deeper into the nature and properties of Christian perfection by viewing it in every possible light. We compared it again and again with the Word of God on the one hand, and the experience of the children of God on the other. But no disagreement at all remains between our first and our current belief. From the beginning, our understanding of it was to have "the mind which was in Christ,"[61] and to "walk as Christ walked."[62] To be perfect is to have all the mind that was in Christ, and to always walk as he walked. In other words, it is to be inwardly and outwardly devoted to God, completely devoted in heart and life. We have the same conception of it now, with neither addition nor subtraction.

16. The hymns concerning Christian perfection in this hymnal are too numerous to transcribe. I shall cite only a part of three:

Saviour from sin, I wait to prove
That Jesus is thy healing name;

Plant, and root, and fix in me
All the mind that was in thee;
Settled peace I then shall find—
Jesu's is a quiet mind.

Anger I no more shall feel,
Always even, always still;
Meekly on my God reclined—
Jesu's is a gentle mind.

I shall suffer, and fulfil
All my Father's gracious will,
Be in all alike resigned—
Jesu's is a patient mind.

Collection, #345, stanzas 5–7

Archbishop James Usher:

a seventeenth-century (1580–1656) churchman and scholar of the Church of Ireland

---

When 'tis deeply rooted here
Perfect love shall cast out fear;
Fear doth servile spirits bind—
Jesu's is a noble mind.

When I feel it fixed within
I shall have no power to sin;
How shall sin an entrance find?
Jesu's is a spotless mind.

I shall nothing know beside
Jesus, and him crucified;
I shall all to him be joined—
Jesu's is a loving mind.

Collection, #345, stanzas 8–10

To lose, when perfected in love,
    Whate'er I have, or can, or am;
I stay me on thy faithful word,
"The servant shall be as his Lord."

Answer that gracious end in me
    For which thy precious life was given;
Redeem from all iniquity,
    Restore, and make me meet for heaven.
Unless thou purge my every stain,
Thy suffering and my faith is vain.

Didst thou not die, that I might live,
    No longer to myself but thee?
Might body, soul, and spirit give
    To Him who gave himself for me?
Come then, my Master and my God,
Take the dear purchase of thy blood.

Thy own peculiar servant claim,
    For thy own truth and mercy's sake;
Hallow in me thy glorious name;
    Me for thine own this moment take;
And change and thoroughly purify;
Thine only may I live and die.

Chose from the world, if now I stand,
    Adorn'd with righteousness divine;
If, brought into the promised land,
    I justly call the Saviour mine;

The sanctifying Spirit pour,
    To quench my thirst and wash me clean,
Now, Saviour, let the gracious shower
    Descend, and make me pure from sin.

Purge me from every sinful blot:
    My idols all be cast aside:
Cleanse me from every evil thought,
    From all the filth of self and pride.

The hatred of the carnal mind
    Out of my flesh at once remove:
Give me a tender heart, resign'd,
    And pure, and full of faith and love.

O that I now, from sin released,
    Thy word might to the utmost prove,
Enter into thy promised rest;
    The Canaan of thy perfect love!

Now let me gain perfection's height!
  Now let me into nothing fall;
Be less than nothing in my sight,
  And feel that Christ is all in all.

Lord, I believe, thy work of grace
  Is perfect in the soul;
His heart is pure who sees thy face,
  His spirit is made whole.

From every sickness, by thy word,
  From every foul disease,
Saved, and to perfect health restored,
  To perfect holiness:

He walks in glorious liberty,
  To sin entirely dead:
The Truth, the Son hath made him free,
  And he is free indeed.

Throughout his soul thy glories shine,
  His soul is all renew'd,
And deck'd in righteousness divine,
  And clothed and fill'd with God.

This is the rest, the life, the peace,
  Which all thy people prove;
Love is the bond of perfectness,
  And all their soul is love.

O joyful sound of gospel grace!
  Christ shall in me appear;
I, even I, shall see his face,
  I shall be holy here!

He visits now the house of clay,
  He shakes his future home; —
O would'st thou, Lord, on this glad day,
  Into thy temple come!

Come, O my God, thyself reveal,
  Fill all this mighty void;
Thou only canst my spirit fill:
  Come, O my God, my God!

Fulfil, fulfil my large desires,
  Large as infinity!
Give, give me all my soul requires,
  All, all that is in thee!

Endnotes

1. Luke 3:9; Acts 15:9
2. Psalm 84:7
3. 2 Corinthians 3:18, NRSV
4. 2 Corinthians 3:17, NRSV
5. Romans 8:2
6. 1 John 5:18; John 8:36
7. 2 Corinthians 3:5, NRSV
8. Philippians 2:13, NRSV
9. See John 14:10.
10. "This is too strong. Our Lord Himself desired ease in pain. He asked for it, only with resignation: 'Not as I will,' I desire, 'but as Thou wilt.'" (John Wesley)
11. Matthew 6:10, NRSV
12. "This is far too strong. See the Sermon on Wandering Thoughts." (John Wesley)
13. "Frequently this is the case, but only for a time." (John Wesley)
14. See 1 John 2:20.
15. "It may be so for a time, but not always." (John Wesley)
16. "Sometimes they have no need; at other times they have." (John Wesley)
17. "Sometimes they do not; at other times they do, and that grievously." (John Wesley)
18. Philippians 4:7, NRSV
19. 1 Peter 1:8, NRSV
20. Ephesians 4:30
21. 2 Timothy 4:8; "Not all who are saved from sin. Many of them have not attained it yet." (John Wesley)
22. 1 Peter 1:7
23. 1 Peter 1:6, NRSV
24. Romans 14:17, NRSV
25. Romans 6:9
26. Romans 5:1
27. Romans 5:2
28. Romans 5:5
29. See 1 Peter 4:12.
30. Romans 8:17
31. Ephesians 4:24
32. Hebrews 4:9
33. 2 Corinthians 6:2
34. Galatians 6:10, NRSV
35. See Ephesians 4:15-16.
36. 1 Corinthians 9:27
37. Philippians 2:5
38. 1 John 2:6
39. Psalm 24:4
40. 2 Corinthians 7:1, NRSV
41. 1 John 2:10, NRSV
42. 1 John 3:9
43. Job 8:20; Ephesians 4:13
44. Ezekiel 36:25, NRSV
45. 1 Thessalonians 5:23
46. 1 John 1:5, 7
47. Galatians 2:19b-20, NRSV
48. 1 Peter 1:15
49. Matthew 22:37
50. Mark 12:30
51. Matthew 22:39
52. Matthew 5:44
53. Colossians 3:12, NRSV
54. 1 Thessalonians 1:3, NRSV
55. Colossians 3:17, NRSV
56. Matthew 6:10
57. 1 Thessalonians 5:23
58. Romans 12:1
59. 1 Peter 2:9
60. Hebrews 12:23
61. Philippians 2:5
62. 1 John 2:6

17. On Monday, June 25, 1744, our First **Conference** began. Six clergymen and all our preachers were present. On Tuesday morning we seriously considered the doctrine of sanctification, also known as perfection. The questions asked and the substance of the answers given, are as follows:

QUESTION. What does it mean to be sanctified?
ANSWER. To be restored in the image of God, "in righteousness and true holiness" (Ephesians 4:24).

Q. What is implied in being a perfect Christian?
A. Loving God with all our heart, and mind, and soul.
   (Deuteronomy 6:5)

Q. Does this imply that all inward sin is taken away?
A. Undoubtedly. Otherwise, how can it be said that we are
   "saved from all our uncleannesses?" (Ezekiel 36:29)

Our Second Conference began August 1, 1745. The next morning we spoke of sanctification as follows:

Q. When does inward sanctification begin?
A. In the moment a person is justified. (Sin yet remains.
   Indeed, the seed of all sin remains until a person is sanctified throughout.) From the moment of justification a
   believer gradually dies to sin and grows in grace.

Q. Is sanctification usually given shortly before death?
A. It is not given to those who do not expect it sooner.

Q. But may we expect it sooner?
A. Why not? We grant (1) that most believers we have
   known were not sanctified until near death; (2) that few
   of those to whom Saint Paul wrote his epistles were sanctified at that time; and (3) that it is likely that Saint Paul
   himself was not sanctified at the time he wrote his epistles. Nonetheless, all these things do not prove that we
   may not be so today.

Q. How should we preach sanctification?
A. Preach it rarely to those who are not seeking after it. To

conference: a three- to four-day meeting of the Methodist preachers with John Wesley. Important issues of theology, practice, and organization were discussed. Quarterly conferences were held usually in November, February, and May in different parts of England for those able to attend. The annual conference was held in London during August. All preachers—lay and clergy—were expected to attend the annual conference. Conferencing helped to galvanize the Methodists.

To get a sense of what happened at the early Methodist conferences, read "Minutes of Several Conversations Between the Rev. Mr. Wesley and Others From the Year 1744 to the Year 1789," in *The Works of John Wesley.*

> Sin in me, the inbred foe,
>   Awhile subsists in chains;
> But thou all thy power shalt show,
>   And slay its last remains;
>
> Thou hast conquered my desire,
>   Thou shalt quench it with thy blood;
> Fill me with a purer fire,
>   And make me all like God.
>
> *Collection,* #349, stanza 5

33

those who are, preach it frequently. Present sanctification as the promise it is, grace from God, always drawing rather than driving.

Our Third Conference began Tuesday, May 13, 1746. We carefully read over the minutes of the two preceding conferences to see if anything needed to be edited or changed upon more careful consideration. But we could find no reason to change anything that we had agreed upon before.

Our Fourth Conference began on Tuesday, June 16, 1747. Because several persons were present who did not believe the doctrine of perfection, we agreed to examine it from the foundation. To begin the discussion, this question was asked:

Q. How much is accepted by our brothers who differ from us with regard to entire sanctification?
A. They grant,
　(1) that every one must be entirely sanctified at the time of death;
　(2) that until then a believer grows in grace daily and comes nearer and nearer to perfection;
　(3) that we should be constantly striving toward it and encouraging all others to do the same.

Q. What do we allow them?
A. We grant,
　(1) that many of those who have died in the faith, indeed most of those we have known, were not perfected in love until a little before their death;
　(2) that the term *sanctified* is constantly applied by Saint Paul to all that were justified;
　(3) that by the term *sanctified* alone he rarely, if ever, means "saved from all sin";
　(4) that, consequently, it is not accurate to use the term *sanctified* in that way without adding modifiers such as *wholly* or *entirely*;
　(5) that the biblical writers speak consistently of, or to, those who were justified, but rarely of, or to, those who were wholly sanctified;[1]
　(6) that, consequently, it is necessary for us to speak steadily about justification, but more rarely,[2] "at least in full and explicit terms, about entire sanctification."

Q. What then is the point where we divide?
A. It is this: Should we expect to be saved from all sin before the time of death?

Q. Is there any clear Scripture promise that God will save us from all sin?
A. There is: "God shall redeem Israel from all its sins" (Psalm 130:8). This is expressed more fully in the prophecy of Ezekiel: "I will sprinkle clean water upon you, and you shall be clean from all your uncleannesses,

and from all your idols. . . . I will save you from all your uncleannesses" (36:25, 29, NRSV). No promise can be more clear. The apostle clearly refers to this in his exhortation: "Since we have these promises, beloved, let us cleanse ourselves from every defilement of body and of spirit, making holiness perfect in the fear of God" (2 Corinthians 7:1, NRSV). Equally clear and precise is that ancient promise: "The LORD your God will circumcise your heart and the heart of your descendants, so that you will love the LORD your God with all your heart and with all your soul" (Deuteronomy 30:6, NRSV).

Q. But are there any corresponding claims to be found in the New Testament?

A. There are. They are written in plain language: "The Son of God was revealed for this purpose, to destroy the works of the devil" (1 John 3:8b, NRSV)—"the works of the devil," without any limitation or restriction; but all sin is the work of the devil. Parallel to this is Saint Paul's assertion: "Christ loved the church and gave himself up for her, in order to make her holy by cleansing her with the washing of water by the word, so as to present the church to himself in splendor, without a spot or wrinkle or anything of the kind—yes, so that she may be holy and without blemish" (Ephesians 5:25b-27, NRSV).

He makes a similar assertion in Romans 8:3-4, "God sent his Son, that the righteousness of the law might be fulfilled in us, who walk not after the flesh, but after the Spirit."

Q. Does the New Testament provide any more reasons to expect to be saved from all sin?

A. Certainly it does, in those prayers and commands that are equivalent to the strongest assertions.

Q. What prayers do you mean?

A. I mean the prayers for entire sanctification. If there were no such thing, they would be simple mockery of God. Here are some examples:

(1) "Deliver us from evil" (Matthew 6:13). Now, when this is done, when we are delivered from all evil, there can be no sin remaining.

(2) "I ask not only on behalf of these, but also on behalf of those who will believe in me through their word, that they may all be one. As you, Father, are in me and I am in you, may they also be in us, . . . I in them and you in me, that they may become completely one (or be made perfect in one)" (John 17:20-21, 23, NRSV).

(3) "I bow my knees before the Father, from whom every family in heaven and on earth takes its name. I pray that, according to the riches of [God's] glory, . . . you may be strengthened in your inner being with power through his Spirit, and that Christ may dwell in your hearts through faith, as you are being rooted and

Jesus, thine all-victorious love
  Shed in my heart abroad!
Then shall my feet no longer rove,
  Rooted and fixed in God.

Love only can the conquest win,
  The strength of sin subdue
(Mine own unconquerable sin),
  And form my soul anew.

Love can bow down the stubborn neck,
  The stone to flesh convert;
Soften, and melt, and pierce, and break
  An adamantine heart.

Collection, #351, stanzas 4–6

grounded in love. I pray that you may have the power to comprehend, with all the saints, what is the breadth and length and height and depth, and to know the love of Christ that surpasses knowledge, so that you may be filled with all the fullness of God" (Ephesians 3:14-19, NRSV).

(4) "May the God of peace himself sanctify you entirely; and may your spirit and soul and body be kept sound and blameless at the coming of our Lord Jesus Christ" (1 Thessalonians 5:23, NRSV).

Q. What command is there?

A. (1) "Be perfect, therefore, as your heavenly Father is perfect" (Matthew 5:48, NRSV).

(2) "You shall love the Lord your God with all your heart, and with all your soul, and with all your mind" (Matthew 22:37, NRSV). If the love of God fills up the heart, no sin can reside there.

Q. But how does it appear that this is to be done before the time of death?

A. (1) The very nature of a command is that it is given to the living and not to the dead. Therefore, "You shall love God with all your heart," cannot mean, "You shall do this when you die." Rather, it means you shall do it while you live.

(2) From explicit passages of Scripture:

a. "For the grace of God has appeared, bringing salvation to all, training us to renounce impiety and worldly passions, and in the present age to live lives that are self-controlled, upright, and godly, while we wait for the blessed hope and the manifestation of the glory of our great God and Savior, Jesus Christ. He it is who gave himself for us that he might redeem us from all iniquity and purify for himself a people of his own who are zealous for good deeds" (Titus 2:11-14, NRSV).

b. "He has raised up a mighty savior for us," to perform "the mercy promised to our ancestors, . . . the oath that he swore to our ancestor Abraham, to grant us that we, being rescued from the hands of our enemies, might serve him without fear, in holiness and righteousness before him all our days" (Luke 1:69, 72, 73-75, NRSV).

Q. Is there any example in Scripture of people who had been perfected in love?

A. Yes. Saint John, and all those of whom he says, "Love has been perfected among us in this: that we may have boldness on the day of judgment, because as he is, so are we in this world" (1 John 4:17, NRSV).

Q. Can you show an example of such a person living today? Where is he or she that is perfect in the way you describe?

O that in me the sacred fire
  Might now begin to glow,
Burn up the dross of base desire,
  And make the mountains flow!

O that it now from heaven might fall,
  And all my sins consume!
Come, Holy Ghost, for thee I call,
  Spirit of burning, come!

Refining fire, go through my heart,
  Illuminate my soul;
Scatter thy life through every part,
  And sanctify the whole.

Collection, #351, stanzas 7–9

A. One might answer to some that ask this, "If I knew one here, I would not tell you. For you do not inquire out of love. You are like Herod—you only seek the young child to slay it."[3]

But more directly we answer: There are many reasons why there should be few, if any, indisputable examples. What misfortunes would this bring on the person who would be set as a mark for all to shoot at! And how unprofitable would it be to opponents! "If they do not listen to Moses and the prophets," Christ and his apostles, "neither will they be convinced even if someone rises from the dead."[4]

Q. Are we not inclined to have a secret aversion to any who say they are saved from all sin?

A. It is possible that we may, for several reasons:
   (1) partly from a concern for the good of souls who may be hurt if those in question are not what they claim to be;
   (2) partly from a kind of unexpressed envy of those who speak of higher attainments than our own; and
   (3) partly from our natural slowness and resistance to believe the works of God.

Q. Why may we not continue in the joy of faith until we are perfected in love?

A. Why indeed, since holy grief does not quench this joy, since even while we are under the cross, while we deeply share of the sufferings of Christ, we may rejoice with joy unspeakable.

In these extracts may be found the judgment of me and my brother, along with that of all the preachers in **connexion** with us in the years 1744–1747. I do not remember even one dissenting voice in any of these conferences. But whatever doubts anyone had when we met were all removed before we parted.

18. In the year 1749 my brother printed two volumes of "Hymns and Sacred Poems." Because I did not see these before they were published, there were some things in them that I did not approve of. But I approved completely of the principal hymns on this point, a few verses of which are provided here:

> Come, Lord, be manifested here,
>   And all the devil's works destroy;
> New, without sin, in me appear,
>   And fill with everlasting joy:
> Thy beatific face display;
> Thy presence is the perfect day.

> Swift to my rescue come,
> Thy own this moment seize;

Sorrow and sin shall then expire,
  While, entered into rest,
I only live my God t'admire—
  My God forever blest.

No longer then my heart shall mourn,
  While purified by grace
I only for his glory burn,
  And always see his face.

My steadfast soul, from falling free,
  Shall then no longer move;
But Christ be all the world to me,
  And all my heart be love.

Collection, #351, stanzas 10–12

---

connexion: the network of Methodist societies served by the Wesley brothers and the preachers. This connexion was a covenant community that pooled its resources to support the preachers and for ministry, and to be under John Wesley's pastoral oversight as a cleric of the Church of England.

Gather my wand'ring spirit home,
    And keep in perfect peace.

Suffer'd no more to rove
    O'er all the earth abroad,
Arrest the pris'ner of thy love,
    And shut me up in God!

Thy pris'ners release, Vouchsafe us thy peace;
And our sorrows and sins in a moment shall cease.
That moment be now! Our petition allow,
Our present Redeemer and Comforter thou!

From this inbred sin deliver;
    Let the yoke Now be broke;
        Make me thine for ever.

Partner of thy perfect nature,
    Let me be Now in thee
        A new, sinless creature.

Turn me, Lord, and turn me now,
To thy yoke my spirit bow;
Grant me now the pearl to find
Of a meek and quiet mind.

Calm, O calm my troubled breast;
Let me gain that second rest:
From my works for ever cease,
Perfected in holiness.

Come in this accepted hour,
    Bring thy heavenly kingdom in!
Fill us with the glorious power,
    Rooting out the seeds of sin.

Come, thou dear Lamb, for sinners slain,
    Bring in the cleansing flood;
Apply, to wash out every stain,
    Thine efficacious blood.

O let it sink into our soul
    Deep as the inbred sin:
Make every wounded spirit whole,
    And every leper clean!

Pris'ners of hope, arise,
  And see your Lord appear:
Lo! on the wings of love he flies,
  And brings redemption near.

Redemption in his blood
  He calls you to receive:
"Come unto me, the pard'ning God:
  Believe," he cries, "believe!"

Jesus, to thee we look,
  Till saved from sin's remains,
Reject the inbred tyrant's yoke,
  And cast away his chains.

Our nature shall no more
  O'er us dominion have:
By faith we apprehend the power,
  Which shall for ever save.

Jesu, our life, in us appear,
  Who daily die thy death:
Reveal thyself the finisher;
  Thy quick'ning Spirit breathe!

Unfold the hidden mystery,
  The second gift impart;
Reveal thy glorious self in me,
  In every waiting heart.

In Him we have peace, In Him we have power!
Preserved by his grace Throughout the dark hour,
In all our temptation He keeps us, to prove
His utmost salvation, His fulness of love.

Pronounce the glad word, And bid us be free!
Ah, hast thou not, Lord, A blessing for me?
The peace thou hast given, This moment impart,
And open thy heaven, O Love, in my heart!

A second edition of these hymns was published in 1752 without any other alteration than that of a few literal mistakes.

I have provided these extended extracts in order to convey, beyond all doubt, that both my brother and I affirmed to this day:

(1) that Christian perfection is the love of God and our neighbor that leads to deliverance from all sin;

(2) that this is received only by faith;

(3) that it is given instantaneously, in one moment;

(4) that we are to expect it, not at death, but every moment. That now is the acceptable time, now is the day of salvation.[5]

Endnotes

1. "That is, to those alone and not others. But they speak to them almost continually together with others." (John Wesley)

2. "More rarely, I allow, but yet in some places very frequently, strongly, and explicitly." (John Wesley)

3. See Matthew 2:1-18.

4. Luke 16:31, NRSV

5. See 2 Corinthians 6:2.

19. At the Conference of 1759, perceiving some danger that a diversity of opinions could cause confusion and damage within our ministry, we again devoted considerable time to serious reflection upon this doctrine. Not long after the conference I published *Thoughts on Christian Perfection*. It was prefaced with the following declaration:

> The following tract is by no means designed to gratify the curiosity of anyone. It is not intended to prove the doctrine in question. It is not directed against those who refute and ridicule it. It does not answer the numerous objections against it, which may be raised even by serious seekers. All I intend here is simply to declare what my beliefs are on this point. I will explain what Christian perfection is and is not, according to my understanding. I will also add a few practical observations and directions pertaining to the subject.
>
> Because these thoughts were initially thrown together by way of question and answer, I let them continue in the same form. They are the same that I have maintained for more than twenty years.

QUESTION. What is Christian perfection?

ANSWER. Christian perfection is loving God with all our heart, mind, soul, and strength. This implies that no passions contrary to love remain in the soul. It means that all thoughts, words, and actions are governed by pure love.

Q. Do you affirm that this perfection excludes all infirmities, ignorance, and mistake?

A. I continually affirm quite the contrary, and have always done so.

Q. But how can every thought, word, and work be governed by pure love while, at the same time, the person is subject to ignorance and mistake?

A. I see no contradiction here. A person may be filled with pure love and still be prone to mistake. Indeed I do not expect to be freed from actual mistakes until this mortal puts on immortality. I believe this to be a natural consequence of the soul's dwelling in bodies of flesh and blood. After all, our thinking is dependent upon bodies and organs that are subject to injury and disease. They are

---

What! never speak one evil word!
  Or rash, or idle, or unkind?
O how shall I, most gracious Lord,
  This mark of true perfection find?

Thy sinless mind in me reveal,
  Thy Spirit's plenitude impart,
And all my spotless life shall tell
  Th'abundance of a loving heart.

Saviour, I long to testify
  The fullness of thy gracious power;
O might thy Spirit the blood apply
  Which bought for me the peace—
    and more!

Forgive, and make my nature whole,
  My inbred malady remove;
To perfect health restore my soul,
  To perfect holiness and love.

Collection, #353

Gaston Jean Baptiste de Renty:
(1611–1649) a highborn Frenchman turned ascetic (see definition below) whose writings and life influenced Wesley. Like Wesley, de Renty was very much influenced by à Kempis's *The Imitation of Christ*.

asceticism: a lifestyle in which followers renounce material comforts and lead lives of austere self-discipline, especially as an act of religious devotion

iron girdle: a device worn around the waist by ascetic monks as a means of self-discipline for prayer and attention to the Word of God. De Renty's desire to discipline his body and mind to the will of Christ lead him to the ascetic practice of wearing an iron girdle. Wesley believed that such extreme measures are mistaken because they lead to self-loathing. This, in his mind, would be counter to the will of Christ because we are to love not only *as* Christ loves but also *whom* he loves, their bodies and their souls. To loathe the self is to loathe that which Christ loves.

merits of Christ: the redeeming work of Christ on the cross through which all the world receives the gift of salvation by grace through faith

Christ in his priestly office: one of the three offices Christ fulfills: Prophet, Priest, and King. The priestly office is that of mediator with the Father through which we receive assurance that our sins are forgiven. In his priestly office Christ draws us to a new relationship with God and keeps us with God.

See the sidebar on page 87 for more information about the offices of Christ.

fragile and unreliable. Therefore, until this perishable body shall have put on imperishability, we cannot avoid sometimes thinking wrong.[1]

But we may carry this thought further yet. A mistake in judgment may possibly cause a mistake in practice. For instance: **Mr. de Renty**'s mistake regarding the nature of **asceticism**, arising from misapplication of education, resulted in the practical mistake of his wearing an **iron girdle**. There may be a thousand more such instances, even in those who are in the highest state of grace. Yet, in those for whom every word and action springs from love, such a mistake is not properly a sin. However, it cannot bear the rigor of God's justice but needs the atoning blood of Christ.

Q. What was the judgment of all our brethren who met at Bristol in August of 1758?
A. It was expressed in these words:
   (1) Every person is subject to mistake as long as he or she lives.
   (2) A mistake in opinion may result in a mistake in practice.
   (3) Every such mistake is a transgression of the perfect law. Therefore,
   (4) Every such mistake, were it not for the blood of atonement, would expose one to eternal damnation.
   (5) It follows that those who are most perfect have constant need of the **merits of Christ**, especially for their actual transgressions. They may say for themselves, as well as for their brethren, "Forgive us our trespasses."[2]

This easily accounts for what might otherwise seem to be utterly mysterious: the fact that those who are not offended when we speak of the highest degree of love will not grant the possibility of living without sin. The reason is that they know all human beings are subject to mistake in practice and in judgment. But they do not understand, or do not see, that this is not sin if love is the source of action.

Q. Does a person living without sin continue to need a Mediator? Does he or she cease to need **Christ in his priestly office**?
A. Far from it. None feel their need of Christ like these. None so entirely depend upon him. For Christ does not give life to the soul apart from, but in and with, himself. Consequently, his words are equally true for all people in whatever state of grace they are: "As the branch cannot bear fruit by itself unless it abides in the vine, neither can you unless you abide in me. . . . Apart from me you can do nothing."[3]

We need Christ at all times because
(1) All the grace we receive is a free gift from him.
(2) We receive it as his work, acknowledging the price he paid.

(3) We have this grace not only *from* Christ but *in* Christ. For our perfection is not like that of a tree, which flourishes by the sap derived from its own root. Rather, it is like that of a branch that bears fruit when united to the vine. But when severed from the vine it dries up and withers.

(4) All our blessings—material, spiritual, and eternal—depend on his intercession for us. This is one branch of his priestly office upon which we always depend.

(5) The best of people continue to need Christ in his priestly office. They need him to atone for their omissions, their shortcomings, their mistakes in judgment and practice, and their various defects. For these are all deviations from the perfect law and, consequently, need an atonement. However, according to the words of Saint Paul, we understand that these are not properly sins. For he says in Romans 13:10 (NRSV), "Love does no wrong to a neighbor; therefore, love is the fulfilling of the law." With this in mind, mistakes and any failings that necessarily flow from the corruptible state of the human body are not contrary to love. Therefore, according to Scriptural definition, they are not sin.

To explain myself a little further on this point:

(1) All transgressions need the atoning blood of Christ. This includes sins as they are properly understood (voluntary transgressions of a known law) and so-called sins (those involuntary transgressions of a divine law, known and unknown).

(2) I believe there is no perfection in this life exempt from these involuntary transgressions. This is so because they are a natural consequence of the ignorance and mistakes that characterize human mortality.

(3) Therefore, *sinless perfection* is a phrase I never use, in order to avoid the appearance of contradicting myself.

(4) I believe that a person filled with the love of God is still subject to these involuntary transgressions.

(5) You may call such transgressions sins, if you please. I do not, for the reasons mentioned above.

Q. What advice would you give to those who do, and those who do not, call them sins?

A. Let those who do not call them sins never think that they or any others are able to stand before God's infinite justice without the mediating work of Christ. Such belief is either the deepest ignorance or the highest arrogance and presumption.

Let those who do call them sins beware how they confuse these **faults** with **actual sins**.

But how will they avoid it? How will faults be distinguished from actual sins if they are all indiscriminately called sins? I fear that if people begin to call faults and mistakes sins, then sins would be considered consistent with perfection. This cannot be.

> Show me, as my soul can bear,
>   The depth of inbred sin,
> All the unbelief declare,
>   The pride that lurks within;
> Take me, whom thyself hast bought,
>   Bring into captivity
> Every high aspiring thought
>   That would not stoop to thee.
>
> *Collection*, #348, stanza 4

actual sins vs. faults/mistakes:
Wesley makes a crucial distinction between actual sins and human faults or mistakes. Sins are voluntary transgressions of God's commandments (see Exodus 20:1-17, Matthew 22:34-40, Mark 12:28-34, Luke 10:25-37, and John 13:34). In other words, a person sins when he or she willfully disobeys a known law. Faults or mistakes, on the other hand, are unknowing violations of God's commands and are not properly regarded to be sins. Wesley is arguing that people who are perfected in love do not commit sins but, by virtue of their humanity, are subject to faults and mistakes.

Jesus, the gift divine I know,
  The gift divine I ask of thee;
That living water now bestow,
  Thy Spirit and thyself on me.
Thou, Lord, of life the fountain art:
Now let me find thee in my heart!

Thee let me drink, and thirst no more
  For drops of finite happiness;
Spring up, O well, in heavenly power,
  In streams of pure, perennial peace,
In peace, that none can take away,
In joy, which shall forever stay.

Father, on me the grace bestow,
  Unblameable before thy sight,
Whence all the streams of mercy flow;
  Mercy, thy own supreme delight,
To me, for Jesu's sake impart,
And plant thy nature in my heart.

Thy mind throughout my life be shown,
  While listening to the wretch's cry,
The widow's and the orphan's groan,
  On mercy's wings I swiftly fly
The poor and helpless to relieve,
My life, my all for them to give.

Thus may I show thy Spirit within,
  Which purges me from every stain;
Unspotted from the world and sin
  My faith's integrity maintain,
The truth of my religion prove
By perfect purity and love.

Collection, #354

Q. But how can a predisposition to mistake be consistent with perfect love? Is not a person who is perfected in love under its influence every moment? Can any mistake flow from pure love?
A. I answer,
   (1) Many mistakes may exist together with pure love;
   (2) Some may accidentally flow from it. I mean, love itself may incline us to mistake. The pure love of our neighbor, springing from the love of God, thinks no evil, believes and hopes all things.[4] Now, this very temperament, unsuspicious, ready to believe and hope the best of all people, may cause us to think some people to be better than they really are. Here then is a clear mistake accidentally flowing from pure love.

Q. How shall we avoid setting perfection too high or too low?
A. By keeping to the Bible, and setting it just as high as the Bible does. Perfection is nothing higher and nothing lower than this: the pure love of God and human beings. In other words, loving God with all our heart and soul, and our neighbor as ourselves. It is love governing the heart and life, running through all our tempers, words, and actions.

Q. Suppose one had attained perfection in love, would you advise him or her to speak of it?
A. At first, perhaps, one would hardly be able to refrain because the fire would be so hot within. The desire to declare the loving kindness of the Lord would carry one away like a torrent. But later one might refrain, and then it would be advisable to refrain from speaking of it to those who do not know God. It would most likely only provoke them to contradict and blaspheme you. It would also be advisable to refrain from speaking of it to others without having some particular reason or some good in view. Even then one should take particular care to avoid all appearance of boasting and to speak with the deepest humility and reverence, giving all the glory to God.

Q. But wouldn't it be better to be entirely silent, to not speak of it at all?
A. By silence one might avoid many crosses that will naturally and necessarily follow if one simply declares, even among believers, what God has worked in one's soul.

But one could not be silent with a clear conscience, for undoubtedly he ought to speak. People do not light a candle to put it under a bushel; neither does the all-wise God. God does not raise such a monument of power and love to hide it from all humankind. Rather, God intends it as a general blessing to those who are simple of heart. God's aim thereby, is not only the happiness of that individual person but the stirring and encouraging of others to follow after the same blessing. God's will is "that many shall see it" and rejoice "and put their trust in the Lord."[5] Nor does anything under heaven more arouse the desires of those who are justified than to converse with those whom they believe to have experienced a still higher salvation. This places that salvation in full view and increases their hunger and thirst for it. This is an advantage that would be entirely lost had the person so saved buried himself in silence.

Q. But is there no way to prevent these crosses that usually fall on those who speak of being perfected in love?

A. It seems they cannot be entirely prevented, as long as so much of human nature remains, even in believers. But something could be done if the preacher in every place would
(1) talk freely with all those who speak thus; and,
(2) work to prevent the unjust or unkind treatment of those in whom there is positive and reasonable proof.

Q. What is reasonable proof? How may we be certain that one is saved from all sin?

A. Unless it should please God to endow us with the miraculous discernment of spirits, we cannot infallibly know who is thus saved (or even who is justified). But we understand the following to be sufficient proof to any reasonable person. Such proof would leave little room to doubt either the truth or depth of the work:
(1) if we had clear evidence of exemplary behavior for some time before this supposed change. This would give us reason to believe that he would not "lie for God" but would speak neither more nor less than he felt.
(2) if he gave a clear account of the time and manner in which the change took shape, with sound speech that could not be reproved; and,
(3) if it appeared that all his subsequent words and actions were holy and irreproachable.

The short of the matter is this:
(1) I have abundant reason to believe that this person will not lie.
(2) This person testifies before God, "I feel no sin, but all love. I pray, rejoice, and give thanks without ceasing, and I have as clear an inward witness that I am fully renewed, as that I am justified."

Now, if I cannot contradict this clear testimony, I should reasonably believe it. It serves nothing to object by saying something like, "But I know he is quite mistaken in several things." For it has been allowed that all who are human are subject to mistake, and that a mistake in judgment may sometimes cause a mistake in practice. However, great care must be taken so that this concession may not be misused. For instance: Even one who is perfected in love may be mistaken with regard to another person, and may, for example, believe someone to be more or less blameworthy than he or she really is. For that reason, one may speak with more or less severity than the truth requires. In this sense (though it is not the primary meaning of Saint James), "in many things we

The boundless love that found out me
For every soul of man is free;
  None of thy mercy need despair;
Patient, and pitiful, and kind,
Thee every soul of man may find,
  And, freely saved, thy grace declare.

A vile backsliding sinner, I
Ten thousand deaths deserved to die,
  Yet still by sovereign grace I live!
Saviour, to thee I still look up,
I see an open door of hope,
  And wait thy fullness to receive.

How shall I thank thee for the grace,
The trust I have to see thy face
  When sin shall all be purged away!
The night of doubts and fears is past,
The Morning Star appears at last,
  And I shall see the perfect day.

I soon shall hear thy quick'ning voice,
Shall always pray, give thanks, rejoice
  (This is thy will, and faithful word);
My spirit meek, my will resigned,
Lowly as thine shall be my mind—
  The servant shall be as his Lord.

Collection, #355, stanzas 4–5

offend all."[6] This therefore is not proof at all that the person speaking in this way is not perfect.

Q. But is it not a proof, if he is surprised or fluttered by a noise, a fall, or some sudden danger?

A. It is not. For one may be frightened, tremble, change color, or be otherwise disordered in body while the soul is calmly fixed on God and remains in perfect peace. No, the mind itself may be deeply distressed, exceeding sorrowful, perplexed and pressed down by heaviness and anguish, even to agony, while the heart cleaves to God by perfect love and the will is wholly resigned to him. Was it not so with the Son of God himself? Does any human being endure the distress, anguish, or agony that he sustained? And yet he knew no sin.

Q. But can anyone who has a pure heart prefer pleasing to unpleasing food, or use any pleasure of sense that is not strictly necessary? If so, how do they differ from others?

A. The difference between these and others in taking pleasant food is that

(1) they need none of these things to make them happy. They have a spring of happiness within. They see and love God. For that reason they "rejoice always, and in everything give thanks."[7]

(2) they may use them, but they do not seek them.

(3) they use them sparingly and not for the sake of the thing itself.

This being assumed, we answer directly: Such a one may use pleasing food without the danger that accompanies those who are not saved from sin. He may prefer it to unpleasing, though equally wholesome, food as a means of increasing thankfulness, looking always to God who gives us all things to enjoy in abundance. On the same principle, he may smell a flower, or eat a bunch of grapes, or take any other pleasure that does not lessen but increases his delight in God. Therefore, neither can we say that one perfected in love would be incapable of marriage and of worldly business. If one were called to either, or both, he or she would be more capable than ever. One would be able to do all things without hurry or concern, without any distraction of spirit.

Q. But if two perfect Christians had children, how could the children be born in sin, since there was none in the parents?

A. It is a possible, but not a probable, case. I doubt whether it ever was or ever will be. But ignoring this, I answer: Sin is imposed upon me, not by my mother and father, but by my first parent. "In Adam all died; by the disobedience of one, all were made sinners"[8]—all human beings, without exception, who were in his loins when he ate the forbidden fruit.

We have a remarkable illustration of this in gardening:

O come, and dwell in me,
  Spirit of power within,
And bring the glorious liberty
  From sorrow, fear, and sin.
The seed of sin's disease,
  Spirit of health, remove,
Spirit of finished holiness,
  Spirit of perfect love.

Hasten the joyful day
  Which shall my sins consume,
When old things shall be passed away,
  And all things new become.
Th'original offence
  Out of my soul erase;
Enter thyself, and drive it hence,
  And take up all the place.

I want the witness, Lord,
  That all I do is right,
According to thy will and word,
  Well-pleasing in thy sight.
I ask no higher state;
  Indulge me but in this,
And soon or later then translate
  To my eternal bliss.

Collection, #356

Grafts on a crabapple-stock bear excellent fruit. But sow the seeds of this fruit, and what will be the event? They produce as undiluted, sour crabapples as ever were eaten.

Q. But what does the perfect one do more than others? What does one who is perfected in love do more than the common believers?

A. Perhaps nothing, because the providence of God may have hedged him in by outward circumstances. Perhaps very little, even though he desires and longs to spend and be spent for God; at the least not visibly. He neither speaks many more words nor does many more works. In much the same way, our Lord himself neither spoke many more words nor did so many more, nor so great, works as some of his apostles (see John 14:12).

But what then does this mean? This is no proof that one who is perfect has no more grace than others, and by this God measures the outward work. Hear these words of Jesus: "Truly I tell you, this poor widow has put in more than all of them."[9] Indeed, this poor man, with his few broken words, has spoken more than them all. Indeed, this poor woman, who has given a cup of cold water, has done more than them all. O cease to "judge according to appearance,"[10] and learn to "judge with right judgment!"[11]

Q. But if I feel no power in either his words or prayer, is this not a proof against him?

A. It is not. For that is perhaps your own fault. You are not likely to feel any power in one who is perfect if any of these obstacles lies in the way:

(1) your own deadness of soul. The Pharisees felt no power even in Jesus, about whom it was said, "Never has anyone spoken like this!"[12]

(2) the guilt of some unrepented sin lying upon the conscience;

(3) any kind of prejudice toward him;

(4) your believing that Christian perfection is not attainable in this life;

(5) unwillingness to think or admit that he has attained it;

(6) overvaluing or idolizing him;

(7) overvaluing yourself and your own judgment.

If any of these is the case, what wonder is it that you feel no power in anything he says? But do not others feel it? If they do, your argument falls to the ground. And if they do not, do any of these obstacles lie in their way too? You must be certain of this before you can build any argument upon your belief. Even then your argument will prove nothing more than that grace and gifts do not always go together.

"But he does not live up to my idea of a perfect Christian." Perhaps no one ever did, or ever will. For your idea may go beyond, or at least beside, the Scriptural account. It may include more than the Bible includes, or something

Father, see this living clod,
    This spark of heavenly fire!
See my soul, the breath of God,
    Doth after God aspire.
Let it still to heaven ascend
Till I my Principle rejoin,
    Blended with my glorious End,
    And lost in Love Divine!

Lord, if thou from me hast broke
    The power of outward sin,
Burst this Babylonish yoke
    And make me free within;
Bid my inbred sin depart,
And I thy utmost word shall prove,
    Upright both in life and heart,
    And perfected in love.

God of all-sufficient grace,
    My God in Christ thou art;
Bid me walk before thy face
    Till I am pure in heart;
Till, transformed by faith divine,
I gain that perfect love unknown,
    Bright in all thy image shine,
    By putting on thy Son.

Father, Son, and Holy Ghost,
    In council join again,
To restore thine image, lost
    By frail, apostate man;
O might I thy form express,
Through faith begotten from above,
    Stamped with real holiness,
    And filled with perfect love!

Collection, #357

47

inbred sin: the consequence of original sin. Because of the Fall in Genesis 3, human beings are separated from relationship with God. This separation results in a corruption of all human ability and power. Because of this inbred sin, human beings are incapable of restoring relationship with God. In relation to Christian perfection, inbred sin is the residue of the old nature that Christ reveals to us as we grow in grace and that catches us unawares in times of spiritual vulnerability or weakness. Charles Wesley describes this beautifully in the following hymn stanza:

> Show me, as my soul can bear,
>   The depth of inbred sin,
> All the unbelief declare,
>   The pride that lurks within;
> Take me, whom thyself hast bought,
>   Bring into captivity
>   Every high aspiring thought
>   That would not stoop to thee.

Collection, #348, stanza 4

O God most merciful and true,
  Thy nature to my soul impart;
Stablish with me the covenant new
  And write perfection on my heart.

To real holiness restored,
  O let me gain my Saviour's mind,
And in the knowledge of my Lord
  Fullness of life eternal find.

Collection, #358, stanzas 1–2

---

not found in the Bible. Scriptural perfection is pure love filling the heart and governing all the words and actions. If your idea includes anything more or anything else, it is not Scriptural. It is no wonder, therefore, that a Scripturally perfect Christian does not come up to your standard.

I fear many stumble on this stumbling block. They include as many ingredients as they please in their idea of one that is perfect. But these are products of their own imagination and not according to Scripture. Then they readily deny anyone to be such when *their* standard is not met. This is why we should take more care to keep the simple, Scriptural account always before us. This is the whole of Scriptural perfection: pure love reigning alone in the heart and life.

Q. When may a person judge himself to have attained this?
A. A person may judge himself or herself to have attained perfection when:
  (1) he or she has been fully convicted of **inbred sin** by a far deeper and clearer conviction than he or she experienced before justification;
  (2) he or she experiences a total death to sin after having experienced a gradual process of outward and inward change;
  (3) there is a complete renewal in the love and image of God so as to "rejoice evermore, to pray without ceasing, and to give thanks in everything."[13]

This is not to say that "to feel all love and no sin" is a sufficient proof. Several have experienced this for a time before their souls were fully renewed. None, therefore, ought to believe that the work is complete until the testimony of the Spirit is added. It is through the Spirit that their entire sanctification is witnessed as clearly as their justification.

Q. But why is it that some imagine that they are entirely sanctified when in reality they are not?
A. It is for this reason: They do not take into account *all* the preceding marks. Rather, they consider either only part of them, or others that are ambiguous. But I know no instance of a person who is attentive to them all and is yet deceived in this matter. I believe that there can be none in the world.

If, after justification, a person is deeply and fully convinced of inbred sin, then experiences a gradual death of sin, and then experiences an entire renewal in the image of God, a clear and direct witness of the renewal immensely greater than that forged when he or she was justified, I judge that it is as impossible for this person to be deceived in this as it is for God to lie. If one whom I know to be truthful testifies these things to me, I ought not, without some sufficient reason, reject that testimony.

Q. Is this death to sin and renewal in love gradual or instantaneous?

A. A person may be dying for some time. However, one does not, properly speaking, die until the instant the soul is separated from the body. In that instant one lives the life of eternity. In like manner, one may be dying to sin for some time but is not dead to sin until sin is separated from his soul. In that instant one lives the full life of love. The change undergone when the body dies is of a different kind, and infinitely greater than any we had known before. Indeed, it is impossible to conceive until then. Similarly, the change brought about when the soul dies to sin is of a different kind, and infinitely greater than any before, and more than one can conceive until experiencing it. Yet one still grows in grace, in the knowledge of Christ, in the love and image of God, and will do so not only until death but also to all eternity.

Q. How are we to wait for this change?

A. Do not wait in careless indifference nor in indolent inactivity. We are to wait in vigorous, universal obedience, in a zealous keeping of all the commandments, in watchfulness and painfulness, in denying ourselves and taking up our cross daily. Add to this earnest prayer and fasting, and a close attendance on all the ordinances of God. If anyone dream of attaining it any other way (or of keeping it when it is attained, even when it is received in the largest measure), one deceives his or her own soul. It is true that we receive it by simple faith. But God does not, will not, give that faith unless we seek it with all diligence, in the way that God has ordained.

This consideration may satisfy those who ask why so few have received the blessing. Inquire how many are seeking it in this way, and you have a sufficient answer.

Prayer is especially lacking. Who continues in prayer at the present moment? Who wrestles with God for this very thing? So, "You do not have, because you do not ask. You ask and do not receive, because you ask wrongly,"[14] namely, that you may be renewed before you die. *Before you die*! Will that content you? No, but ask that it may be done now, today, while it is called today. Do not call this "setting God a time." Certainly, today is God's time as well as tomorrow. Make haste, people, make haste! Let

> Thy soul break out in strong desire
> The perfect bliss to prove;
> Thy longing heart be all on fire
> To be dissolved in love!

Q. But may we not continue in peace and joy until we are perfected in love?

A. Certainly we may, for the kingdom of God is not divided against itself. Therefore, let believers not be discouraged from "rejoicing in the Lord always."[15] And yet we may be

> Deepen the wound thy hands have made
>   In this weak, helpless soul,
> Till mercy, with its balmy aid,
>   Descends to make me whole.
>
> The sharpness of thy two-edged sword
>   Enable me t'endure,
> Till bold to say, My hallowing Lord
>   Hath wrought a perfect cure.
>
> I see th'exceeding broad command,
>   Which all contains in one;
> Enlarge my heart to understand
>   The mystery unknown.
>
> O that with all thy saints I might
>   By sweet experience prove
> What is the length, and breadth, and height,
>   And depth of perfect love!
>
> *Collection, #359*

> Give me the enlarged desire,
>   And open, Lord, my soul,
> Thy own fullness to require,
>   And comprehend the whole;
> Stretch my faith's capacity
>   Wider and yet wider still;
> Then, with all that is in thee,
>   My soul forever fill!
>
> *Collection, #361*

sensibly distressed at the sinful nature that still remains in us. It is good for us to have an acute sense of this, and a fervent desire to be delivered from it. But this should only incite us to run every moment more zealously to our strong Helper; the more earnestly to "press forward to the mark, the prize of our high calling in Christ Jesus."[16] And when the sense of our sin abounds most, the sense of his love should abound much more.

Q. How should we treat those who think they have attained perfection?

A. Examine them honestly and exhort them to pray fervently that God would show them all that is in their hearts. The most fervent encouragement to abound in every grace, and the strongest cautions to avoid all evil, are given throughout the New Testament to those who are in the highest state of grace. This should be done with the utmost tenderness, and without any harshness, sternness, or sourness. We should carefully avoid the appearance of anger, unkindness, or contempt. Leave it to Satan to tempt in such a way and to his children to cry out, "Let us examine him with malice and torture, that we may know his meekness and prove his patience." If those who think they have attained perfection are faithful to the grace given, they are in no danger of perishing by this; no, not if they continue to think that they have reached perfection until they are dying.

Q. But what harm is done if they are dealt with harshly?

A. Either they are mistaken, or they are not. If they are, such harsh treatment may destroy their souls. This is neither impossible nor improbable. It may so enrage or so discourage them that they will sink and rise no more.

On the other hand, if they are not mistaken, it may grieve those whom God has not grieved and do much harm to our own souls. For undoubtedly the one that touches them, touches, as it were, the apple of God's eye. If they are indeed full of his Spirit, to behave unkindly or contemptuously to them is doing no little malice to the Spirit of grace. As a result, likewise, we feed and increase in ourselves evil suspicions and many wrong tempers.

For example, what arrogance is this to set ourselves up as inquisitors-general or absolute judges in these deep things of God! Are we qualified for the office? Can we declare, in all cases, how far disorder reaches? What may, and what may not, be its essential ingredients? What may in all circumstances, and what may not, correspond with perfect love? Can we determine precisely how it will influence the appearance, the gesture, the tone of voice? If we can, certainly we are "the people, and wisdom shall die with us."[17]

Jesu, thy boundless love to me
  No thought can reach, no tongue
    declare;
O knit my thankful heart to thee,
  And reign without a rival there!
Thine wholly, thine alone I am;
Be thou alone my constant flame!

O grant that nothing in my soul
  May dwell, but thy pure love alone!
O may thy love possess me whole,
  My joy, my treasure, and my crown;
Strange flames far from my heart
    remove—
My every act, word, thought, be love.

O Love, how cheering is thy ray!
  All pain before thy presence flies!
Care, anguish, sorrow, melt away,
  Where'er thy healing beams arise;
O Jesu, nothing may I see,
Nothing desire or seek but thee!

Collection, #362, stanzas 1–3

Q. But if they are displeased at our not believing them, is not this a full proof against them?

A. It depends upon the nature of the displeasure. If they are angry, it is a proof against them. If they are grieved, it is not. They ought to be grieved if we disbelieve a genuine work of God and accordingly deprive ourselves of the advantage we might have received from it. Also, we may easily mistake this grief for anger. After all, the outward expressions of both are similar.

Q. But is it not good to discover those who mistakenly believe they have attained perfection?

A. It is best to do it by mild, loving examination. But it is not good to triumph even over such findings. If we find such an instance, it is extremely wrong to rejoice as if we had found a great prize. Should we not rather grieve, to be deeply concerned, to let our eyes be filled with tears? Here is one who seemed to be a living proof of God's power to save to the extreme. But, alas, it is not as we hoped. This one is weighed in the balance and found wanting! How can this be a matter of joy? Should we not rejoice a thousand times more if we can find nothing but pure love?

But if one is deceived, what then? It is a harmless mistake while one feels nothing but love in his or her heart. It is a mistake that generally demonstrates great grace and a high degree of both holiness and happiness. This should be a matter of true joy to all that are sincere of heart—not the mistake itself but the height of grace that for a time arises from it. I rejoice that this soul is always happy in Christ, always full of prayer and thanksgiving. I rejoice that this soul feels no unholy temper, but feels the pure love of God continually. And I will rejoice if sin is suspended until it is totally destroyed.

Q. Is there no danger then in being thus deceived?

A. Not at the time that one feels no sin. There was danger before, and there will be again when one comes into fresh trials. But as long as one feels nothing but love guiding all thoughts, words, and actions, that one is in no danger. Such a one is not only happy but is safe "under the shadow of the Almighty."[18] For God's sake, let one such as this continue in that love as long as he or she can. In the meantime, you may do well to warn of the danger that will be if the love grows cold and sin revives. Warn also about the danger of casting away hope and supposing that because one has not attained perfection yet, he or she never will.

Q. But what if none have attained perfection yet? What if all who think they have are deceived?

A. Convince me of this and I will preach it no more. But understand me correctly: I do not build any doctrine on any particular person. Any one may be deceived, and I am not moved. But if there are none made perfect yet, God has not sent me to preach perfection.

Unwearied may I this pursue,
  Dauntless to the high prize aspire;
Hourly within my soul renew
  This holy flame, this heavenly fire;
And day and night be all my care
To guard this sacred treasure there.

My Saviour, thou thy love to me
  In shame, in want, in pain hast
    showed;
For me on the accursed tree
  Thou pouredst forth thy guiltless
    blood.
Thy wounds upon my heart impress,
Nor aught shall the loved stamp
    efface.

More hard than marble is my heart,
  And foul with sins of deepest stain;
But thou the mighty Saviour art,
  Nor flowed thy cleansing blood in
    vain.
Ah, soften, melt this rock, and may
Thy blood wash all these stains away!

Collection, #362, stanzas 4–6

O that I as a little child
  May follow thee and never rest
Till sweetly thou hast breathed thy mild
  And lowly mind into my breast!
Nor ever may we parted be
Till I become one spirit with thee.

Still let thy love point out my way
  (How wondrous things thy love
    hath wrought!)
Still lead me, lest I go astray,
  Direct my word, inspire my thought;
And if I fall, soon may I hear
Thy voice, and know that love is near.

In suffering be thy love my peace,
  In weakness be thy love my power;
And when the storms of life shall cease,
  Jesu, in that important hour,
In death as life be thou my guide,
And save me, who for me hast died.

Collection, #362, stanzas 7–9

Take a parallel case for example: For many years I have preached, "There is a peace of God that passes all understanding."[19] Convince me that this word is no longer true, that in all these years none have attained this peace, that there is no living witness of it today, and I will preach it no more.

"O, but several people have died in that peace." Perhaps so, but I want living witnesses. Indeed, I cannot be entirely certain that any person is a witness. But if I were certain there are none, I would have to abandon this doctrine.

"You misunderstand me. I believe some who died in this love enjoyed it long before their death. But I was not certain that their former testimony was true until some hours before they died." You did not have complete certainty then. You might have had a reasonable certainty before. Such a certainty might have enlivened and comforted your own soul and answered all other Christian purposes. Supposing there is any living witness, any honest person may have such a certainty as this simply by talking one hour with that person in the love and fear of God.

Q. But what does it mean, whether any have attained it or not, seeing so many Scriptures witness for it?

A. If I were convinced that none in England had attained what has been so clearly and strongly preached by so many preachers, in so many places, and for so long a time, I should be clearly convinced that we had all mistaken the meaning of those Scriptures. Therefore, for the time to come, I too must teach that "sin will remain until death."

Endnotes

1. See 1 Corinthians 15:53.
2. Matthew 6:12
3. John 15:4-5, NRSV
4. See 1 Corinthians 13:7.
5. Psalm 40:3
6. James 3:2
7. 1 Thessalonians 5:16, 18
8. 1 Corinthians 15:22; Romans 5:19
9. Luke 21:3, NRSV
10. John 7:24
11. John 7:24, NRSV
12. John 7:46, NRSV
13. 1 Thessalonians 5:16-18
14. James 4:2-3, NRSV
15. Philippians 4:4
16. Philippians 3:14
17. Job 12:2
18. Psalm 91:1
19. Philippians 4:7

20. In the year 1762, there was a great increase of the work of God in London. Many who previously had no interest in any of these things were deeply convinced of their lost condition. Many found redemption in the blood of Christ. Not a few backsliders were healed. And a considerable number of people believed that God had saved them from all sin. Easily anticipating that Satan would be striving to sow weeds among the wheat,[1] I took great pains to warn them of the danger, particularly with regard to **pride** and **enthusiasm**.

While I stayed in town, I had reason to hope they remained both humble and sensible. But almost as soon as I was gone, enthusiasm broke in. Two or three began to take their own imaginations for impressions from God, and from there they began to believe that they will never die. They caused much noise and confusion while working to bring others into the same belief. Soon after, the same people along with a few more developed other excesses: thinking that they could not be tempted, that they would feel no more pain, and that they had the gift of prophecy and of discerning of spirits.

When I returned to London in autumn, some of them stood corrected while others were beyond instruction. In the meantime I was flooded with criticism from almost every quarter. The Londoners were unhappy because I was restraining them on all occasions. Others, outside of London, were angry because I did not check them. However, the hand of the Lord was not hindered. More and more sinners were convicted, some were converted to God almost daily, and others were enabled to love him with all their heart.

21. About this time, a friend at some distance from London wrote to me as follows:

> Do not be unduly alarmed that Satan sows weeds among the wheat of Christ. It has always been so, especially on any extraordinary outpouring of his Spirit. And it will always be so, until Satan is chained up for a thousand years.[2] Until then, he will always imitate and work to counteract the work of the Spirit of Christ.
>
> One lamentable effect of this has been that a world, which is always asleep in the arms of the evil one, has ridiculed every work of the Holy Spirit.

pride: having too high an opinion of the self and its powers. Pride is a danger to the soul because it causes one to believe that he or she is self-sufficient and does not need God. Pride leads to self-centeredness, which leads ultimately to rebellion against God and rejection of grace.

enthusiasm: a religious fervor that is often coupled with powerful emotional experience. This experience often leads to ardent religious devotion that tends toward arrogance, self-righteousness, and fanatacism. For this reason, Wesley later warns that pride often leads to enthusiasm.

The early Methodists were often accused of being enthusiasts because of the emotional response that accompanied society and class meetings and because of the disciplined lives supported by the class meeting and bands.

real Christians: those who have the form and the power of Christian religion. They keep the General Rules and practice the means of grace. They earnestly love God with all their heart, soul, mind, and strength, and they love their neighbors as themselves. Real Christians do all in their power to grow in that love.

The contrasting term Wesley used was *almost Christians*, those who have the form without the power. They attend the services of the church but do not participate in the means of grace or seek actively to grow in their love of God and neighbor.

Saviour from sin, I wait to prove
 That Jesus is thy healing name,
To lose, when perfected in love,
 Whate'er I have, or can, or am;
I stay me on thy faithful word,
The servant shall be as his Lord.

Answer that gracious end in me,
 For which thy precious life was given:
Redeem from all iniquity,
 Restore, and make me meet for
  heaven.
Unless thou purge my every stain,
Thy suffering and my faith are vain.

Didst thou not in the flesh appear
 Sin to condemn and man to save?
That perfect love might cast out fear?
 That I thy mind in me might have,
In holiness show forth thy praise,
And serve thee all my spotless days?

Didst thou not die that I might live
 No longer to myself, but thee?
Might body, soul, and spirit give
 To him who gave himself for me?
Come then, my Master, and my God!
Take the dear purchase of thy blood.

Collection, #364, stanzas 1–4

But what can <u>real Christians</u> do? Why, if they would act worthy of themselves, they should (1) pray that every deluded soul may be delivered; (2) strive to reclaim them in the spirit of humility; (3) lastly, take the utmost care, both by prayer and watchfulness, that the delusion of others may not lessen their zeal in pursuing that universal holiness of soul, body, and spirit "without which no man shall see the Lord."[3]

Indeed this complete new creation is mere insanity to an insane world. But it is, nevertheless, the will and wisdom of God. May we all seek after it!

But some who completely affirm this doctrine are frequently guilty of limiting the Almighty. God dispenses gifts exactly as God pleases. Therefore, it is neither wise nor modest to affirm that a person must be a believer for any length of time before he or she is capable of receiving a high degree of the Spirit of holiness.

God's usual method is one thing, but God's sovereign will is another. God has wise reasons both for speeding up and slowing God's work. Sometimes God comes suddenly and unexpectedly and sometimes not until we have sought for God for a long time.

Indeed it has been my belief for many years, that one great reason people make so little improvement in the spiritual life is their own coldness, negligence, and unbelief. And yet I speak here of believers.

May the Spirit of Christ give us a right judgment in all things and "fill us with all the fullness of God"[4] so that we may be "perfect and complete, wanting nothing."[5]

22. About the same time, five or six honest enthusiasts predicted the world was to end on the 28th of February. I immediately opposed them by every possible means, both in public and private. I preached specifically upon the subject, both at West-Street and Spitalfields. I warned the society again and again, and spoke personally to as many as I could. I saw the fruit of my labor. They made few converts—I believe barely thirty in our whole society. Nevertheless, they made much noise, gave significant aid and comfort to those who opposed me, and greatly increased both the number and courage of those who opposed Christian perfection.

23. Some questions, now published by one of these opponents, caused a plain man to write the following:

Queries humbly proposed to those who deny that perfection is attainable in this life:
(1) Has there not been a larger measure of the Holy Spirit given under the Gospel than under the Jewish dispensation? If not, in what sense was the Spirit not given before Christ was glorified? (John 7:39)
(2) Was that "glory which followed the sufferings of Christ" (1 Peter 1:11) an external glory or an internal glory, namely, the glory of holiness?

(3) Has God anywhere in Scripture commanded us more than God has promised to us?

(4) Are the promises of God concerning holiness to be fulfilled in this life or only in the next?

(5) Is a Christian under any laws other than those that God promises to "write in our hearts"? (Jeremiah 31:33 and Hebrews 8:10)

(6) In what sense is "the righteousness of the law fulfilled in those who walk not after the flesh but after the Spirit"? (Romans 8:4)

(7) Is it impossible for anyone in this life to "love God with all heart, and mind, and soul, and strength"? (Mark 12:30) And is the Christian under any law that is not fulfilled in this love?

(8) Does the soul's going out of the body bring about its purification from **indwelling sin**?

(9) If so, is it not something else, not "the blood of Christ, which cleanses" it "from all sin"?[6]

(10) If Christ's blood cleanses us from all sin while the soul and body are united, does that not happen in this life?

(11) If Christ's blood cleanses us from all sin when the union of soul and body ceases, does that not happen in the next life? And is this not too late?

(12) If Christ's blood cleanses us from all sin in the moment of death, then what is the state of the soul when it is neither in the body nor out of it?

(13) Has Christ taught us anywhere to pray for what he never intends to give?

(14) Has he not taught us to pray, "Thy will be done on earth, as it is done in heaven" (Matthew 6:10)? Is it not done perfectly in heaven?

(15) If so, has he not taught us to pray for perfection on earth? Does he not then intend to give it?

(16) Did not Saint Paul pray according to the will of God when he prayed that the Thessalonians might be "sanctified wholly, and preserved" (in this world, not the next, unless he was praying for the dead), "blameless in body, soul, and spirit, unto the coming of Jesus Christ"?[7]

(17) Do you sincerely desire to be freed from indwelling sin in this life?

(18) If you do, didn't God give you that desire?

(19) If so, did God give it to you in order to mock you, since you believe it is impossible it should ever be fulfilled?

(20) If you don't even have enough sincerity to desire to be freed from indwelling sin, are you not disputing about matters too high for you?

(21) Do you ever pray that God would **"cleanse the thoughts of your heart, that"** you **"may perfectly love God"**?

(22) If you neither desire what you ask, nor believe it attainable, do you not pray as a fool prays?

God help you to consider these questions calmly and completely!

indwelling sin: the same as inbred sin. See sidebar on page 48.

> Quickened with our immortal Head,
>   Who daily, Lord, ascend with thee,
> Redeemed from sin, and free indeed,
>   We taste our glorious liberty.
>
> Saved from the fear of hell and death,
>   With joy we seek the things above;
> And all thy saints the Spirit breathe
>   Of power, sobriety, and love.
>
> Power o'er the world, the fiend, and sin,
>   We through thy gracious Spirit feel;
> Full power the victory to win,
>   And answer all thy righteous will.
>
> Pure love to God thy members find,
>   Pure love to every soul of man;
> And in thy sober, spotless mind,
>   Saviour, our heaven on earth we gain.
>
> *Collection*, #407

"cleanse the thoughts . . .": This is a reference to the "Collect for Purity" from the weekly eucharist liturgy of the *Book of Common Prayer*. See sidebar on page 23.

Memorial accounts such as this one of Jane Cooper were common among the early Methodists. Similar accounts regularly appeared in *The Arminian Magazine*, published by Wesley beginning in 1778.

Their role was to be an inspiration to others, that they may change and live lives of holiness.

24. Near the end of this year, God called to himself that burning and shining light, Jane Cooper. As she was both a living and a dying witness of Christian perfection, it is appropriate to include here a brief account of her death, with one of her own letters containing a plain and sincere telling of how it pleased God to work that great change in her soul:

May 2, 1761

I believe while memory remains in me, gratitude will continue. From the time you preached on <u>Galatians 5:5</u>, I saw clearly the true state of my soul. That sermon described my heart and what it wanted to be, namely truly happy. You read Mr. M—'s letter, and it described the religion I desired. From that time the prize appeared in view, and I was enabled to follow hard after it. I was kept watching unto prayer, sometimes in much distress, at other times in patient expectation of the blessing.

For some days before you left London, my soul lingered on a promise I had applied to me in prayer: "The Lord whom you seek shall suddenly come to his temple."[8] I believed he would, and that he would sit there as a refiner's fire.

The Tuesday after you went, I thought I could not sleep unless he fulfilled his word that night. I never knew as I did then the force of these words: "Be still, and know that I am God."[9] I became nothing before God, and enjoyed perfect calmness in my soul. I knew not whether God had destroyed my sin, but I desired to know so that I might praise God. Yet I soon found the return of unbelief and, being burdened, I groaned.

On Wednesday I went to London and sought the Lord without ceasing. I promised I would praise him if he would save me from sin. I could part with all things so that I might win Christ. But I found all these pleas to be worth nothing, and that if Christ saved me, it must be freely, for his own name's sake.

On Thursday I was tempted so much that I thought of destroying myself or never again conversing with the people of God. And yet I had no doubt of God's pardoning love, but,

'Twas worse than death my God to love,
And not my God alone.

On Friday my distress was deepened. I tried to pray and could not. I went to Mrs. D., who prayed for me and told me it was the death of nature. I opened the Bible on, "The fearful and unbelieving shall have their part in the lake that burns with fire and brimstone."[10] I could not bear it. I opened again, on Mark 16:6-7: "Do not be alarmed; you are looking for Jesus of Nazareth, . . . go, tell his disciples . . . that he is going ahead of you to Galilee; there you will see him" (NRSV). I was encouraged, and enabled to pray, believing I should see Jesus at home.

I returned that night, and found Mrs. G. She prayed for me; and the <u>Predestinarian</u> had no plea but, "Lord, thou art no respecter of persons."[11] He proved he was not by blessing me. I was in a moment enabled to lay hold on Jesus Christ, and found salvation by simple faith. He assured me that the Lord, the King, was in the midst of me and that I should see evil no more. I now blessed him who had visited and redeemed me and had become my "wisdom, righteousness, sanctification, and redemption."[12] I saw Jesus altogether lovely and knew that he was mine in all his offices. Glory be to him. Christ now reigns in my heart without a rival. I find no will but his. I feel no pride, nor any affection but for him.

I know it is by faith I stand. Watching in prayer must be the guard of faith. I am happy in God this moment, and I believe for the next. I have often read the chapter you mention, 1 Corinthians 13, and compared my heart and life with it. In so doing, I feel my shortcomings and the need I have of the atoning blood. Yet I dare not say, I do not feel a measure of the love described there, though I am not all I shall be. I desire to be lost in that "love which passes knowledge."[13] I see "the just shall live by faith,"[14] and to me, who is less than the least of all saints, is this grace given. If I were an archangel, I would veil my face before him and let silence speak his praise!"

The following account is given by one who was an eyewitness to what she relates:

(1) In the beginning of November she seemed to have a premonition of what was coming upon her and frequently used to sing these words:

> When pain o'er this weak flesh prevails,
> With lamb-like patience arm my breast.

And when she sent word to me to let me know she was ill, she wrote in her note, "I suffer the will of Jesus. All he sends is sweetened by his love. I am as happy as if I heard a voice say,

> For me my elder brethren stay,
> And angels beckon me away,
> And Jesus bids me come!"

(2) Upon my telling her, "I cannot choose life or death for you," she said, "I asked the Lord that if it was God's will, I might die first. And he told me you should survive me and that you should close my eyes." When we realized that she had smallpox, I said to her, "My dear, you will not be frightened if we tell you what your disorder is." She said, "I cannot be fearful at God's will."

(3) The disease was soon very heavy upon her, but her faith was strengthened that much more. Tuesday, November 16, she said to me, "I have been worshiping before the

predestinarian: a person who believes in the doctrine of predestination, which teaches that God has foreordained all things, especially that God has elected certain souls to eternal salvation and others to eternal punishment

---

O all that pass by, To Jesus draw near,
He utters a cry; Ye sinners, give ear!
From hell to retrieve you, He spreads
   out his hands;
Now, now to receive you He graciously stands.

If any man thirst, And happy would be,
The vilest and worst May come unto me;
May drink of my spirit (Excepted is
   none),
Lay claim to my merit, And take for
   his own.

Whoever receives The life-giving word,
In Jesus believes, His God and his Lord,
In him a pure river Of life shall arise,
Shall in the believer Spring up to the
   skies.

My God and my Lord! Thy call I obey;
My soul on thy word Of promise I stay;
Thy kind invitation I gladly embrace;
Athirst for salvation, Salvation by
   grace

O hasten the hour! Send down from
   above
The spirit of power, Of health, and of
   love;
Of filial fear, Of knowledge and grace,
Of wisdom, of prayer, Of joy, and of
   praise:

The spirit of faith, Of faith in thy
   blood,
Which saves us from wrath, And
   brings us to God,
Removes the huge mountain Of
   indwelling sin,
And opens a fountain That washes us
   clean.

Collection, #3

throne in a glorious manner. My soul was listening to God!" I said, "Did the Lord give you any particular promise?" "No," she replied, "it was all

> That sacred awe that dares not move,
> And all the silent heaven of love.

(4) On Thursday, upon my asking, "What have you to say to me?" she said, "Nay, nothing but what you know already: God is love." I asked, "Have you any particular promise?" She replied, "I do not seem to want any. I can live without. I shall die a lump of deformity but shall meet you all-glorious. In the meantime, I shall still have fellowship with your spirit."

(5) Mr. M. asked what she thought was the most excellent way to walk in and what were its chief obstacles. She answered, "The greatest obstacle is generally from the natural personality. It was mine to be reserved, to be very quiet, to suffer much and to say little. Some may think one way more excellent, and some another; but the thing is to live in the will of God. For some months past, when I have been particularly devoted to this, I have felt such a guidance of God's Spirit. The anointing I have received from the Holy One has so taught me of all things that I did not need any human to teach me, except as this anointing teaches."

(6) On Friday morning she said, "I believe I shall die." She then sat up in her bed and said, "Lord, I bless you, that you are ever with me, and all you have is mine. Your love is greater than my weakness, greater than my helplessness, greater than my unworthiness. Lord, you say to corruption, 'You are my sister!' Glory be to you, O Jesus; you are my Brother. Let me comprehend with all saints the length, and breadth, and depth, and height of thy love! Bless these," (some that were present). "Let them be every moment used in all things as you would have them to be."

(7) Some hours later, it seemed as if the agonies of death were just coming upon her, but her face was full of smiles of triumph, and she clapped her hands for joy. Mrs. C said, "My dear, you are more than conqueror through the blood of the Lamb." She answered, "Yes, O yes, sweet Jesus! O death, where is thy sting?" She then lay as in a doze for some time. Afterward she attempted to speak but could not. However, she demonstrated her love by shaking hands with all in the room.

(8) Mr. W then came. She said, "Sir, I did not know that I should live to see you. But I am glad the Lord has given me this opportunity, and likewise power, to speak to you. I love you. You have always preached the strictest doctrine, and I loved to follow it. Do so still, whoever is pleased or displeased." He asked, "Do you now believe you are saved from sin?" She said, "Yes, I have had no doubt of it for many months. That I ever had doubt was because I did not abide in the faith. I now feel I have kept the faith, and 'perfect love casts out all fear.'[15] As to you, the Lord promised me that your latter works should exceed your former, though

---

Us who climb thy holy hill
  A general blessing make;
Let the world our influence feel,
  Our gospel-grace partake:
Grace to help in time of need,
Pour down on sinners from above,
All thy Spirit's fullness shed,
  In showers of heavenly love.

Make our earthy souls a field
  Which God delights to bless;
Let us in due season yield
  The fruits of righteousness;
Make us trees of paradise,
Which more and more thy praise
  may show,
Deeper sink, and higher rise,
  And to perfection grow.

Collection, #412

God of all-redeeming grace,
  By thy pardoning love compelled,
Up to thee our souls we raise,
  Up to thee our bodies yield;
Thou our sacrifice receive,
  Acceptable through thy Son,
While to thee alone we live,
  While we die to thee alone.

Meet it is, and just, and right,
  That we should be wholly thine,
In thy only will delight,
  In that blessed service join:
O that every work and word
  Might proclaim how good thou art!
Holiness unto the Lord
Still be wrote upon our heart!

Collection, #415

I do not live to see it. I have been a great enthusiast, as they term it, these six months, but never lived so near to the heart of Christ in my life. You, sir, desire to comfort the hearts of hundreds by following that simplicity your soul loves."

(9) To one who had received the love of God under her prayer, she said, "I feel I have not followed a cunningly devised fable, for I am as happy as I can live. Do press on, and do not stop short of the mark." To Miss M—s she said, "Love Christ. He loves you. I believe I shall see you at the right hand of God. But as one star differs from another star in glory, so shall it be in the resurrection. I charge you, in the presence of God, meet me in that day all-glorious within. Avoid all conformity to the world. You are robbed of many of your privileges. I know I shall be found blameless. Do labor to be found by him in peace, without spot."

(10) Saturday morning she prayed nearly as follows: "I know, my Lord, my life is prolonged only to do your will. And though I should never eat or drink more," (she had not swallowed anything for nearly twenty-eight hours) "thy will be done. I am willing to be kept so a year. 'One does not live by bread alone.'[16] I praise you that there is not a shadow of complaining in our streets. In that sense we know not what sickness means. Indeed, Lord, 'Neither life, nor death, nor things present, nor things to come, no, nor any creature, shall separate us one moment from your love.'[17] Bless these, that there may be no lack in their souls. I believe there shall not. I pray in faith."

On Sunday and Monday she was lightheaded, but sensible at times. It then plainly appeared that her heart was still in heaven. One said to her, "Jesus is our mark." She replied, "I have but one mark; I am all spiritual." Miss M said to her, "You dwell in God." She answered, "Altogether." Someone asked her, "Do you love me?" She said, "O, I love Christ. I love my Christ." To another she said, "I shall not long be here. Jesus is precious, very precious indeed." She said to Miss M, "The Lord is very good. He keeps my soul above all." For fifteen hours before she died, she was in strong convulsions. Her sufferings were extreme. One said, "You are made perfect through sufferings." She said, "More and more so." After lying quiet some time, she said, "Lord, thou art strong!" Then, pausing a long time, she uttered her last words, "My Jesus is all in all to me. Glory be to him through time and eternity." After this, she lay still for about half an hour and then expired without a sigh or groan.

Let him to whom we now belong,
  His sovereign right assert,
And take up every thankful song,
  And every loving heart.

He justly claims us for his own,
  Who bought us with a price;
The Christian lives to Christ alone,
  To Christ alone he dies.

Jesus, thine own at last receive!
  Fulfil our heart's desire!
And let us to thy glory live,
  And in thy cause expire.

Our souls and bodies we resign:
  With joy we render thee
Our all, no longer ours, but thine,
  To all eternity.

Collection, #416

Endnotes

1. See Matthew 13:24-30.
2. See Revelation 20:2.
3. Hebrews 12:14
4. Ephesians 3:19
5. James 1:4
6. 1 John 1:7
7. 1 Thessalonians 5:23
8. Malachi 3:1
9. Psalm 46:10
10. Revelation 21:8
11. See Acts 10:34
12. 1 Corinthians 1:30
13. Ephesians 3:19
14. Romans 1:17; Galatians 3:11; Hebrews 10:38
15. 1 John 4:18
16. Matthew 4:4, NRSV
17. Romans 8:38, 39

VI

25. The next year, the number of those who believed they were saved from sin still increasing, I judged it necessary to publish, mainly for their use, *Farther Thoughts on Christian Perfection*:

QUESTION 1. How is "Christ the end of the law for righteousness to every one that believes"? (Romans 10:4)

ANSWER. In order to understand this, you must understand what law is spoken of here. This I understand is (1) the Mosaic law, the whole Mosaic system, which Saint Paul repeatedly speaks of as one, though containing three parts: the political, moral, and ceremonial. (2) The Adamic law was given to Adam in innocence and is properly called "the law of works." This is in substance the same as the angelic law, being common to angels and humans. It required that humans should use, to the glory of God, all the powers with which they were created. Now, they were created free from any defect, either in understanding or affections. The human body was then no impediment to the mind. It did not hinder clearly understanding all things, judging truly concerning them, and reasoning justly, if they reasoned at all. I say "if they reasoned," for possibly they did not. Perhaps they had no need of reasoning until their corruptible bodies pressed down the mind and impaired their natural abilities. Perhaps until then, the mind saw every truth as directly as the eye now sees the light.

Consequently, this law, proportioned to their original powers, required that they should always think, always speak, and always act precisely right, in every possible point. They were very able to do so. God could not but require the service they were able to give.

But Adam fell. His incorruptible body became corruptible and, ever since, it is a clog to the soul and hinders its operations. Consequently, today no human being can understand clearly or judge truly at all times. It is impossible to reason correctly where either the judgment or perception is wrong. Therefore, it is as natural for a human being to mistake as to breathe. A person can no more live without the one than without the other. Consequently, no human is able to perform the service that the Adamic law requires.

1 Corinthians 9:21, NRSV:

"To those outside the law I became as one outside the law (though I am not free from God's law but am under Christ's law) so that I might win those outside the law."

Romans 13:9-10:

"The commandments, 'You shall not commit adultery; You shall not murder; You shall not steal; You shall not covet'; and any other commandment, are summed up in this word, 'Love your neighbor as yourself.' Love does no wrong to a neighbor; therefore, love is the fulfilling of the law."

1 Timothy 1:5:

"But the aim of such instruction is love that comes from a pure heart, a good conscience, and sincere faith."

> Behold the servant of the Lord!
>   I wait thy guiding eye to feel,
> To hear and keep thy every word,
>   To prove and do thy perfect will;
> Joyful from my own works to cease,
> Glad to fulfil all righteousness.
>
> Me if thy grace vouchsafe to use,
>   Meanest of all thy creatures, me,
> The deed, the time, the manner
>   choose,
>   Let all my fruit be found of thee:
> Let all my works in thee be wrought,
> By thee to full perfection brought.
>
> Here then to thee thy own I leave;
>   Mould as thou wilt thy passive clay:
> But let me all thy stamp receive;
>   But let me all thy words obey;
> Serve with a single heart and eye,
> And to thy glory live and die.
>
>   *Collection,* #417, stanzas 1, 2, 4

No human is, of course, obliged to perform it. God does not require it of any human. For Christ is the end of the Adamic, as well as the Mosaic, law. By his death he has put an end to both. He has abolished both the one and the other, with regard to humankind. The obligation to observe either the one or the other is vanished away. Nor is anyone living bound to observe the Adamic more than the Mosaic law.

In place of this, Christ has established another, namely, the law of faith. Not everyone who does, but everyone who believes, now receives righteousness in the full sense of the word. That is, they are justified, sanctified, and glorified.

Q. 2. Are we then dead to the law?

A. We are "dead to the law, by the body of Christ" given for us (Romans 7:4). That is to say, we are dead to the Adamic as well as the Mosaic law. We are completely set free by Christ's death. That law died with him.

Q. 3. How, then, are we "not free from God's law but . . . under Christ's law" (**1 Corinthians 9:21**, NRSV)?

A. While we are no longer under that law, it does not mean that no law applies to us. For God has established another law in its place, the law of faith. We are all under this law through God and through Christ. Both our Creator and our Redeemer require us to keep it.

Q. 4. Is love the fulfilling of this law?

A. Certainly, it is. The whole law under which we now live is fulfilled by love (see **Romans 13:9-10**). Faith working or made active by love is all that God now requires of human beings. God has substituted not sincerity but love in the room of angelic perfection.

Q. 5. How is "love the aim of the commandment" (**1 Timothy 1:5**)?

A. It is the aim of every commandment of God. It is the expected outcome of the whole and every part of the Christian life. The foundation is faith, purifying the heart. The aim is love, preserving a good conscience.

Q. 6. What love is this?

A. It is loving the Lord our God with all our heart, mind, soul, and strength; and loving our neighbor, every human being, as ourselves, as our own souls.[1]

Q. 7. What are the fruits or properties of this love?

A. Saint Paul informs us at length that love is patient. It suffers all the weaknesses of the children of God and all the wickedness of the children of the world. It does so for as long as God pleases. In all, it sees and willingly submits to the hand of God. All the while, it is kind. In all and after all, it suffers; it is soft, mild, tender, benign.

"Love is not envious."[2] It excludes from the heart every kind and degree of envy.

"Love does not act rashly," in a violent, headstrong manner. It does not pass any rash or severe judgment. It "does not behave indecently," is not rude, and does not act out of character.

Love does not seek her own ease, pleasure, honor, or profit. "It is not provoked. It expels all anger from the heart.

"Love thinks no evil," casting out all jealousy, suspicion, and readiness to believe evil. "Love does not rejoice in wrongdoing." Indeed, it weeps at the sin or folly of its bitterest enemies. "But love rejoices in the truth," in the holiness and happiness of every human being.

"Love covers all things," speaks evil of no one, and "believes all things" that tend to the advantage of another's character. It "hopes all things," whatever may lessen the faults that cannot be denied, and it "endures all things" that God can permit, or human beings and devils inflict. This is "the law of Christ, the perfect law, the law of liberty."

This distinction between the "law of faith" (or love) and "the law of works" is neither a subtle nor an unnecessary distinction. It is plain, easy, and intelligible to any common understanding. And it is absolutely necessary for preventing a thousand doubts and fears, even in those who do "walk in love."

Q. 8. But don't we all make mistakes,[3] even the best of us, against this law?

A. In one sense we do not, as long as all our character, thoughts, words, and actions flow from love. But because we live in fallible human bodies, we will be subject to errors in judgment and action. For neither love nor the "anointing of the Holy One"[4] makes us infallible. Therefore, because we are subject to faulty thinking and understanding, we cannot avoid error in many things. These mistakes will frequently give rise to something wrong in our character, words, and actions. For example, we may wrongly judge a person's character and love less than is deserved. This mistake then leads us to speak or act in regard to that person in a way that is contrary to this law.

Q. 9. Do we then not need Christ, even on this point?

A. The holiest of people still need **Christ as their Prophet**, as "the light of the world."[5] He gives them light from moment to moment. All is darkness the instant he withdraws.

They still need **Christ as their King**, because God does not give them a supply of holiness. But unless they receive a supply every moment, nothing but unholiness remains.

They still need **Christ as their Priest**, to make atonement for their holy things. Even perfect holiness is acceptable to God only through Jesus Christ.

Father, Son, and Holy Ghost,
    One in Three, and Three in One,
As by the celestial host,
    Let thy will on earth be done:
Praise by all to thee be given,
Glorious Lord of earth and heaven!

Vilest of the sinful race,
    Lo! I answer to thy call;
Meanest vessel of thy grace,
    Grace divinely free for all;
Lo! I come to do thy will
All thy counsel to fulfil.

If so poor a worm as I
    May to thy great glory live,
All my actions sanctify,
    All my words and thoughts receive;
Claim me, for thy service claim
All I have, and all I am.

Take my soul and body's powers;
    Take my memory, mind, and will;
All my goods, and all my hours,
    All I know, and all I feel!
All I think, or speak, or do;
Take my heart: but make it new!

Now, O God, thy own I am,
    Now I give thee back thy own:
Freedom, friends, and health, and fame,
    Consecrate to thee alone;
Thine I live, thrice happy I!
Happier still if thine I die.

Father, Son, and Holy Ghost,
    One in Three, and Three in One,
As by the celestial host
    Let thy will on earth be done:
Praise by all to thee be given,
Glorious Lord of earth and heaven!

Collection, #418

Christ as Prophet, Christ as King, Christ as Priest:
For more on the offices of Christ, see sidebar on page 87.

Q. 10. May not, then, the very best of people adopt the dying Martyr's confession: "I am in myself nothing but sin, darkness, hell. But you are my light, my holiness, my heaven"?

A. Not exactly. But the best of people may say, "You are my light, my holiness, my heaven. Through my union with you, I am full of light, of holiness, and happiness. But if I were left to myself, I would be nothing but sin, darkness, hell."

The best of people need Christ as their Priest, their Atonement, and their Advocate with the Father. They need Christ not only because the continuance of their every blessing depends on his death and intercession, but because of their falling short of the law of love. This is true for every living person. Those of you who feel all love compare yourselves with the preceding description. Weigh yourselves in this balance and see if you are not lacking in many areas.

Q. 11. But if all this is consistent with Christian perfection and "sin is the transgression of the law,"[6] then that perfection is not freedom from sin, because those who are perfect break the very law they are under. Besides, they need the atonement of Christ. He is the atonement of nothing but sin. Therefore, is the term *sinless perfection* appropriate?

A. It is not worth arguing. But let us look at how the people in question need the atonement of Christ. They do not need him to reconcile them to God again, for they are reconciled. They do not need him to restore the favor of God, but to continue it. He does not obtain pardon for them anew, but "always lives to make intercession for them"; and "by a single offering he has perfected for all time those who are sanctified" (Hebrews 7:25; 10:14, NRSV).

For failing to properly consider this, some deny that they need the atonement of Christ. Indeed, very few. I do not remember finding five of them in England. Of the two (atonement or perfection), I would first give up perfection, but we need not give up either one or the other. The perfection I advocate, "Love rejoicing evermore, praying without ceasing, and in everything giving thanks,"[7] is very consistent with the atonement of Christ. If any advocate a perfection that is not consistent with the atonement of Christ, they must look carefully at what they advocate.

Q. 12. Does then Christian perfection imply anything more than sincerity?

A. Not if you mean by that word love filling the heart, expelling pride, anger, desire, and self-will; rejoicing always; praying without ceasing; and in everything giving thanks. But I suspect few use *sincerity* in this sense. Therefore, I think the old word is best.

A person may be sincere who has all natural dispositions (tempers), pride, anger, lust, self-will. But one is not perfect until the heart is cleansed from these and all its other corruption.

To make this point a little more clear: I know many that love God with all their heart. God is their one desire, their one delight, and they are continually happy in God. They love their neighbor as themselves. They feel as sincere, fervent, and constant a desire for the happiness of everyone, good or bad, friend or enemy, as for their own happiness. They "rejoice always, pray without ceasing, and in everything give thanks."[8] Their souls are continually streaming up to God in holy joy, prayer, and praise. This is a point of fact, and this is plain, sound, scriptural experience.

But even these souls live in a shattered body. They are so oppressed by its brokenness that they cannot always act as they would like, by thinking, speaking, and acting correctly. Because they lack better bodily organs, they must at times think, speak, or act wrong. Indeed, they do this not through a defect of love but through a defect of knowledge. While this is the case, they fulfil the law of love in spite of that defect and its consequences.

Yet because, even in this case, there is not a full conformity to the perfect law, the most perfect do for this very reason need the blood of atonement and may properly say for themselves, as well as for their brothers and sisters, "Forgive us our trespasses."[9]

Q. 13. But if Christ has put an end to that law, why is atonement needed for breaking it?
A. Look at the reason he has put an end to it, and the difficulty vanishes. If it were not for the enduring merit of his death and his constant intercession for us, that law would still condemn us. Therefore, we still need atonement for every transgression.

Q. 14. But can one who is saved from sin be tempted?
A. Yes, for Christ was tempted.

Q. 15. However, what you call temptation I call the corruption of my heart. How will you distinguish one from the other?
A. In some cases it is impossible to distinguish without the direct witness of the Spirit. But in general one may distinguish in this manner:
- If someone commends me, here is a temptation to pride. But instantly my soul is humbled before God, and I feel no pride. I am as sure of this as I am that pride is not humility.
- If a man strikes me, here is a temptation to anger. But my heart overflows with love, and I feel no anger at all. I can be as sure of this as I am that love and anger are not the same.
- If a woman solicits me, here is a temptation to lust. But in that instant I shrink back and feel no desire or lust at

Send down thy likeness from above,
  And let this my adorning be;
Clothe me with wisdom, patience, love,
  With lowliness and purity,
Than gold and pearls more precious far,
And brighter than the morning star.

Lord, arm me with thy Spirit's might,
  Since I am called by thy great name;
In thee let all my thoughts unite,
  Of all my works be thou the aim;
Thy love attend me all my days,
And my sole business be thy praise.

Collection, #419, stanzas 5–6

witness of the Spirit: the assurance of salvation given when one accepts the grace of God in Jesus Christ and trusts in him and only him as Savior and Lord. Wesley experienced such a witness at Aldersgate Street, London, on May 24, 1738.

fruit of the Spirit: love, joy, peace, patience, kindness, generosity, faithfulness, gentleness, and self-control (Galatians 5:22-23)

relative change: Justifying grace restores a person to right relationship with God. Sins are forgiven. The gift of faith is given and received. Forgiveness, repentance, and faith are the beginnings of the new, right relationship with God. Grace enables the person to turn away from sin and toward God. Justifying grace brings us face-to-face with God, much like a flower follows the sun across the sky on a clear day. (See Romans 3:21-26.)

real change: Justification (relative change) is the beginning of sanctification, or perfection in love (real change). Paul describes this change in 2 Corinthians 5:17: "So if anyone is in Christ, there is a new creation: everything old has passed away; see, everything has become new!" Imagine what happens to a caterpillar encased in its cocoon. The caterpillar experiences a real change. It emerges from the cocoon as a butterfly, an entirely new creation that leads an entirely new way of life. God's grace works through faith in and with us to bring about such a real change (Ephesians 2:8). (See also Ephesians 4:14-16; Philippians 2:12-13; 1 John 4:17-21.)

all. I can be as sure of this as I am that my hand is cold or hot.

This is how it is if I am tempted by a present object. It is just the same if, when it is absent, the devil recalls a commendation, an injury, or a woman to my mind. In that instant the soul repels the temptation and remains filled with pure love.

And the difference is even more clear when I compare my present state with my past, in which I felt temptation and corruption too.

Q. 16. But how do you know that you are sanctified and saved from your inbred corruption?

A. I can know it in the same way that I know I am justified. "By this we know that we abide in him and he in us, because he has given us of his Spirit."[10]

We know it first by the **witness** and then by the **fruit of the Spirit**. When we were justified, the Spirit bore witness with our spirit that our sins were forgiven. In the same way, when we were sanctified the Spirit bore witness that our sins were taken away. Indeed, the witness of sanctification is not always clear at first (as neither is that of justification). Neither is it always the same later as it is at first. But like that of justification, it is sometimes stronger and sometimes fainter. Likewise, it is sometimes withdrawn. Yet in general, the latter testimony of the Spirit is both as clear and as steady as the earlier.

Q. 17. Because sanctification is a real change and not, like justification, only a **relative change**, why is this witness of the Spirit needed?

A. Is the new birth only a relative change? Is it not a **real change**? Therefore, if we need no witness of our sanctification because it is a real change, then for the same reason we should need no witness that we are born of, or are the children of, God.

Q. 18. But doesn't sanctification shine by its own light?

A. And doesn't the new birth do the same? Sometimes it does, and so does sanctification. At other times it does not. In the hour of temptation Satan clouds the work of God and injects various doubts and ideas, especially in those who have either very weak or very strong understandings. At such times there is absolute need of that witness, without which the work of sanctification not only could not be discerned but could no longer continue. If it were not for this, the soul could not then abide in the love of God, much less "rejoice always" and "give thanks in everything."[11] In these circumstances, therefore, a direct testimony that we are sanctified is necessary in the highest degree.

Someone may say, "But I have no witness that I am saved from sin. And yet I have no doubt of it." To which I respond, "Very well. As long as you have no doubt, it is enough. But when the doubt comes, you will need that witness."

Q. 19. But what Scripture makes mention of any such thing or gives any reason to expect it?

A. That Scripture, "Now we have received not the spirit of the world, but the Spirit that is from God, so that we may understand the gifts bestowed on us by God" (1 Corinthians 2:12, NRSV).

Now certainly sanctification is one of "the gifts bestowed on us by God." No possible reason can be given why this should be omitted when the apostle says, "We have received . . . the Spirit" for this very purpose, "that we may understand the gifts" thus "bestowed on [or freely given] us."

Is not the same thing implied in that well-known Scripture, "It is that very Spirit bearing witness with our spirit that we are children of God" (Romans 8:16)? Does the Spirit witness this only to those who are children of God in the **lowest sense**? No, but to those also who are such in the **highest sense**. And does he not witness, that they are such in the highest sense? What reason do we have to doubt it?

What if a man were to affirm (as indeed many do) that this witness belongs only to the highest class of Christians? Would you not answer, "The apostle makes no restriction. Therefore, without a doubt it belongs to all the children of God"? And will the same answer not hold if any affirm that it belongs only to the lowest class?

Consider likewise 1 John 5:19: "We know that we are God's children." How? "By the Spirit that God has given us." Even, "Hereby we know that God abides in us." What reason do we have, either from Scripture or reason, to exclude the witness or the fruit of the Spirit from being intended here? By this then also "we know that we are God's children," and in what sense we are so. We know in the same way, whether we are infants, youths, or adults.

Not that I affirm that all youth, or even adults, have this testimony every moment. There may be breaks in the direct testimony that they are thus born of God. But those breaks are fewer and shorter as they grow up in Christ. Some have the testimony of both their justification and their sanctification without any break at all. This, I presume, more might have if they walked humbly and closely with God.

Q. 20. Won't some of them have a testimony from the Spirit that they will not finally fall from God?

A. They may. This belief, that neither life nor death shall separate them from God,[12] far from being harmful, may in some circumstances be extremely useful. These, therefore, we should in no way discourage, but earnestly encourage them to "hold the beginning of their confidence steadfast to the end."[13]

lowest sense, highest sense: Christians in the **lowest sense** are those who have professed faith in Christ but who have not surrendered their will to him. Christians in the **highest sense** are those who have surrendered the will. They have experienced the relational change of justification and the real change of sanctification.

See Sermon 14, "The Repentance of Believers," and Sermon 40, "Christian Perfection," in *The Works of John Wesley.*

Jesus, all-atoning Lamb,
Thine, and only thine I am;
Take my body, spirit, soul,
Only thou possess the whole!

Thou my one thing needful be;
Let me ever cleave to thee;
Let me choose the better part;
Let me give thee all my heart.

Fairer than the sons of men,
Do not let me turn again,
Leave the fountain-head of bliss,
Stoop to creature-happiness.

Whom have I on earth below?
Thee, and only Thee, I know.
Whom have I in heaven but thee?
Thou art all in all to me.

All my treasure is above;
All my riches is thy love.
Who the worth of love can tell?
Infinite, unsearchable!

Thou, O love, my portion art.
Lord, thou know'st my simple heart:
Other comforts I despise—
Love be all my paradise.

Nothing else can I require;
Love fills up my whole desire.
All thy other gifts remove,
Still thou giv'st me all in love.

Collection, #422

Q. 21. But do any have a testimony from the Spirit that they shall never sin?

A. We do not know what God may give to some particular people. But we do not find any general condition described in Scripture from which a person cannot be drawn back to sin. If there were any condition in which this was impossible, it would be that of these who are sanctified, who are "adults in Christ," who "rejoice always, pray without ceasing, give thanks in all circumstances."[14] But it is not impossible for even these to draw back. Those who are sanctified may yet fall and perish (Hebrews 10:29). Even adults in Christ need the warning: "Do not love the world or the things in the world" (1 John 2:15, NRSV). Those who rejoice, pray, and give thanks without ceasing may, nevertheless, "quench the Spirit" (1 Thessalonians 5:16-19). Indeed, even those who are "sealed for the day of redemption" may yet "grieve the Holy Spirit of God" (Ephesians 4:30).

Therefore, although God may give such a witness to some particular persons, it is not to be expected by Christians in general. We believe this because there is no Scripture upon which to base such an expectation.

Q. 22. By what fruit of the Spirit may we "know that we are God's children," even in the highest sense?

A. By love, joy, peace, always abiding within. By invariable endurance, patience, obedience. By gentleness triumphing over all provocation. By goodness, kindness, sweetness, tenderness of spirit. By fidelity, simplicity, godly sincerity. By meekness, calmness, a well-balanced spirit. By temperance, not only in food and sleep, but in all things natural and spiritual.

Q. 23. But what's the big deal about this? Don't we have all this when we are justified?

A. What! Total resignation to the will of God without any mixture of self-will? Gentleness without any touch of anger, even at the moment we are provoked? Love for God without the least love for the world, but in and for God, excluding all pride? Love for humankind, excluding all envy, jealousy, and rash judging? Meekness, keeping the whole soul perfectly calm? And moderation in all things?

You may deny that any ever lived up to this. But do not say all who are justified do.

Q. 24. But some who are newly justified do possess these fruits. What then will you say to these?

A. If they really do, I will say they are sanctified, saved from sin in that moment, and that they need never lose what God has given or feel sin any more.

But certainly this is an exceptional case. It is outside the norm of those that are justified. They feel in themselves more or less pride, anger, self-will, and a heart inclined to backsliding. And until they have gradually subdued these, they are not fully renewed in love.

Jesu, my truth, my way,
My sure, unerring light,
On thee my feeble steps I stay,
Which thou wilt guide aright.

My wisdom and my guide,
My counsellor thou art;
O never let me leave thy side,
Or from thy paths depart!

Collection, #424, stanzas 1–2

Q. 25. But is not this the case of all that are justified? Do they not gradually die to sin and grow in grace until at, or perhaps a little before, death God perfects them in love?

A. I believe this is the case of most, but not all. God usually gives a considerable time for people to receive light, to grow in grace, to do and suffer God's will before they are either justified or sanctified. But God does not always adhere to this. Sometimes God "cuts short God's work." God does the work of many years in a few weeks, or perhaps in a week, a day, an hour. God justifies or sanctifies both those who have done or suffered nothing and those who have not had time for a gradual growth either in light or grace. And, "Am I [God] not allowed to do what I choose with what belongs to me? Or are you envious because I am generous?"[15]

Let's review some facts that do not need to be affirmed over and over and proved by forty passages of Scripture:
- Most people are perfected in love at death.
- There is a gradual work of God in the soul.
- It is a long time, even many years, before sin is destroyed.

All this we know. But we also know that God may, with human cooperation, "cut short God's work" in whatever degree God pleases and complete the usual work of many years in a moment. God does so in many instances, and yet there is a gradual work both before and after that moment. Accordingly, without any contradiction, one may affirm that the work is gradual, and another may affirm that it is instantaneous.

Q. 26. When he writes about being "sealed by the Spirit," does Saint Paul mean anything more than being "renewed in love"?

A. Perhaps in one place, namely <u>2 Corinthians 1:22</u>, he does not mean that much. But in <u>Ephesians 1:13</u> he seems to include both the fruit and the witness in a higher degree than we experience even when we are first "renewed in love." God "seals us with the Spirit of promise"[16] by giving us "the full assurance of hope."[17] This is such a confidence of receiving all the promises of God that it excludes the possibility of doubting. With that Holy Spirit, by universal holiness, the whole image of God is stamped on our hearts.

Q. 27. But how can those who are sealed in this way "grieve the Holy Spirit of God"?

A. Saint Paul tells you very particularly,
- by conversation that is not beneficial, edifying, or likely to minister grace to the hearers;
- by relapsing into bitterness or lack of kindness;
- by wrath, lasting displeasure, or lack of tenderheartedness;
- by anger, however soon it is over, and lack of instantly forgiving one another;

2 Corinthians 1:21-22:
"But it is God who establishes us with you in Christ and has anointed us, by putting his seal on us and giving us his Spirit in our hearts as a first installment" (NRSV).

Ephesians 1:13:
"In him you also, when you had heard the word of truth, the gospel of your salvation, and had believed in him, were marked with the seal of the promised Holy Spirit" (NRSV).

- by bluster or bawling, loud, harsh, rough speaking;
- by evil-speaking, whispering, gossiping, needlessly mentioning the fault of an absent person, even in a soft manner.

Q. 28. What do you think of those in London who seem to have been recently "renewed in love"?

A. There is something very peculiar in the experience of most of them. One would expect that a believer should first be filled with love and then emptied of sin. However, these were emptied of sin first and then filled with love. Perhaps it pleased God to work in this way, to make God's work more plain and undeniable and to distinguish it more clearly from that overflowing love that is often felt even in a justified state.

It seems likewise most consistent with the great promise: "You shall be clean from all your uncleannesses. . . . A new heart I will give you, and a new spirit I will put within you" (Ezekiel 36:25, 26; NRSV).

But I do not think of all of these people in the same way. There is a wide difference between some of them and others. I think that most of them with whom I have spoken have much faith, love, joy, and peace. I believe that some of these are renewed in love and have the direct witness of it. They exhibit the fruit described above in all their words and actions. Now, let any one call this what he or she will. It is what I call perfection.

But some who have much love, peace, and joy do not yet have the direct witness. And others who think they have are, nevertheless, clearly lacking in the fruit. How many I will not say. Perhaps one in ten; perhaps more or fewer. But some are undeniably lacking in patience and Christian obedience. They do not see the hand of God in whatever occurs and cheerfully embrace it. They do not give thanks in everything and rejoice always. They are not happy, at least not always happy. For sometimes they complain. They say this or that is too hard!

Some are lacking in gentleness. They resist evil instead of turning the other cheek. They do not receive reproach or reproof with gentleness. Indeed, they are not able to bear opposition without the appearance, at least, of resentment. If they are reproved or contradicted, though mildly, they do not take it well. They behave with more distance and reserve than they did before. If they are reproved or contradicted harshly they answer it with harshness, with a loud voice, or an angry tone, or in a sharp and surly manner. They speak sharply or roughly when they reprove others and behave roughly to their inferiors.

Some are lacking in goodness. They are not kind, mild, sweet, amiable, soft, and loving at all times in their spirit, in their words, in their look and attitude, in the whole tone of their behavior. They behave this way toward all, high and low, rich and poor, without respect to who it is, particularly to those who are different, to adversaries, and to those of their own household. They do not desire, consider, or seek by every means to make others near them happy. They can see that others are uneasy and not be concerned. Perhaps they make them so, and then wipe their mouths and say, "Why, they deserve it. It is their own fault."

Some are lacking in fidelity. They exhibit a lazy regard for truth, simplicity, and godly sincerity. Their love is rarely without pretense. Something like deception is found in their mouth. To avoid roughness they lean to the other extreme. They are smooth to excess so as seldom to avoid a degree of fawning, or of seeming to mean what they do not.

Some are lacking in meekness, quietness of spirit, composure, evenness of temper. They are up and down, sometimes high, sometimes low. Their mind is not well balanced. Their emotions are not in due proportion—they have too much of one, too little of another, or they are not properly balanced together. Consequently, there is often a clash. Their soul is out of tune and cannot make the true harmony.

Some are lacking in temperance.

- They do not regularly eat the kinds and quantities of food that they know, or should know, would most contribute to good health and stamina.

- Or they are not temperate in sleep. They don't rigorously follow a pattern that is best for body and mind. Otherwise they would regularly go to bed and rise early at the same times each day.

- Or they eat their supper late in the evening. This is good for neither body nor soul.

- Or they neither fast nor abstain.

- Or they prefer preaching, reading, or conversation that gives them temporary joy and comfort rather than that which brings godly sorrow[18] or instruction in righteousness. Such joy is not sanctified. It does not lead to, and end in, the **crucifixion of the heart**. Such faith does not center in God, but rather in itself.

So far all is plain. I believe that you have faith, love, joy, and peace. Yet you who are particularly concerned know for yourself that you each are lacking in one or more of the aspects mentioned above. You are lacking either in patience, gentleness, goodness, fidelity, meekness, or moderation. Let us not then, on either hand, fight about words. In this we clearly agree.

You do not have what I call perfection. If others will call it so, they may. However, hold on to what you have, and earnestly pray for what you have not.

Q. 29. Can those who are perfect grow in grace?
A. Certainly they can, not only in this life but the life to come.

crucifixion of the heart: complete surrender of the heart to God; following Jesus in his admonition to "deny themselves and take up their cross daily and follow me. For those who want to save their life will lose it, and those who lose their life for my sake will save it" (Luke 9:23-24, NRSV).

> O make me all like thee,
>   Before I hence remove!
> Settle, confirm, and stablish me,
>   And build me up in love.
>
> Let me thy witness live,
>   When sin is all destroyed;
> And then my spotless soul receive,
>   And take me home to God.
>
> *Collection*, #424, stanzas 9–10

> O God of peace and pardoning love
> Whose bowels of compassion move
>   To every sinful child of man,
> Jesus, our Shepherd, great and good,
> Who dying bought us with his blood,
>   Thou hast brought back to life again.
> His blood to all our souls apply
> (His blood alone can sanctify
>   Which first did for our sins atone):
> The cov'nant of redemption seal,
> The depth of love, of God, reveal,
>   And speak us perfected in one.
>
> *Collection*, #426, stanza 1

Q. 30. Can they fall from grace?

A. I am certain they can. Reason and experience put this beyond dispute. Previously we thought that one who was saved from sin could not fall. But now we know this is not true. We are surrounded with examples of those who recently experienced all that I mean by perfection. They had both the fruit and the witness of the Spirit. But now they have lost both. No one may ever expect to stand by virtue of anything implied in the nature of Christian perfection. There is no height or strength of holiness from which it is impossible to fall. If there are any who cannot fall, this depends completely upon the promise of God.

Q. 31. Can those who fall from this state recover it?

A. Why not? We have many instances of this also. Indeed, it is very common for people to lose it more than once before they are established in it.

It is therefore to protect the ones who are saved from sin and from every occasion of stumbling that I give the following words of advice. But first I will speak plainly about the work itself.

I consider this ongoing work to be of God and probably the greatest now upon earth. Yet like all others, this work is also mixed with much human frailty. But these weaknesses are far less than might have been expected, and ought to have been joyfully carried by all those who loved and followed after righteousness. That there have been a few weak, excitable people is no dishonor to the work itself. Such behavior is no just ground for accusing a multitude of sober-minded people who are patterns of strict holiness. Yet the opposition is great and the helps are few. This is exactly the opposite of what should have been. By this means, many are prevented from seeking faith and holiness by the false zeal of others. Some who at first began to run well are misled.

Endnotes

1. See Matthew 22:37, 39.
2. See 1 Corinthians 13.
3. See James 3:2.
4. 1 John 2:20
5. John 8:12; 9:5; 11:9
6. 1 John 3:4
7. 1 Thessalonians 5:16-18
8. 1 Thessalonians 5:16-18
9. Luke 11:4a
10. 1 John 4:13, NRSV
11. 1 Thessalonians 5:16, 18
12. See Romans 8:38-39.
13. Hebrews 3:14
14. 1 Thessalonians 5:16-18, NRSV
15. Matthew 20:15, NRSV
16. See Ephesians 1:13.
17. Hebrews 6:11
18. See 2 Corinthians 7:9-11.

Q. 32. What is the first advice that you would give them?

A. Beware of and pray constantly against pride. If God has cast it out, see that it does not return. It is every bit as dangerous as desire. When you think there is no danger, you may slide back into it without notice.

You may say, "Indeed, but I credit all I have to God." You may do so and be proud nevertheless. For it is pride not only to credit anything we have to ourselves, but to think we have what we really do not have. For example, Mr. L— credited all the light he had to God, and so far he was humble. But then he thought he had more light than any man living. This was palpable pride. So you credit all the knowledge you have to God and, in this respect, you are humble. But if you think you have more than you really have, or if you think you are so knowledgeable of God as to no longer need human teaching, then pride is at the door. Yes, you need to be taught, not only by **Mr. Morgan**, one another, **Mr. Maxfield**, or me, but by the weakest preacher in London, yes, by all people. For God sends to us those whom God chooses to send.

Therefore, do not say to any who would advise or correct you, "You are blind. You cannot teach me." Do not say, "This is *your* wisdom, *your* human reason." But calmly discern the thing in the presence of God.

Always remember that much grace does not imply much light. These do not always go together. As there may be much light where there is but little love, so there may be much love where there is little light. The heart has more heat than the eye, and yet it cannot see. God has wisely assembled the members of the body together such that none may say to another, "I have no need of you."[1]

To imagine that none can teach you but those who are themselves saved from sin is a very great and dangerous mistake. Do not entertain that thought for a moment. It would lead you into a thousand other mistakes from which you may never recover. No, supremacy is not founded in grace, as the madmen of the last age talked. Obey and respect "those . . . who have charge of you in the Lord,"[2] and do not think you know better than they. Know their place and your own. Always remember that much love does not imply much light.

Mr. Morgan: James Morgan, one of Wesley's preachers who was associated with Thomas Maxfield

Mr. Maxfield: Thomas Maxfield, a Methodist known for his fanatical teaching and preaching on Christian perfection. Wesley tried on many occasions to correct him but to no avail. Maxfield was also the first Methodist layman to preach. Wesley at first objected but relented when his mother, Susanna, interceded on Maxfield's behalf.

Neglecting to observe this has led some into many mistakes and into the appearance, at least, of pride. Beware of the appearance of pride and of pride itself! Let there "be in you that lowly mind which was in Christ Jesus."[3] And "clothe yourselves with humility."[4] Let it not only fill you but cover you all over. Let modesty appear in all your words and actions. Let all you speak and do show that you are small, humble, and common in your own eyes.

As an example of this, always be ready to own any mistake for which you are responsible. If you have at any time thought, spoken, or acted wrong, do not deny or dodge your responsibility. Never dream that such an admission will hurt the cause of God. Rather, it will further it. Therefore, be open and frank when you are accused of anything. Do not seek either to evade or disguise it. Let it appear just as it is, and you will not hinder, but beautify, the gospel.

Q. 33. What is the second advice you would give those who have fallen from grace?

A. Beware of that child of pride, enthusiasm. Have nothing to do with it! Leave no room for an undisciplined imagination. Do not hastily attribute things to God. Do not easily believe that dreams, voices, impressions, visions, or revelations are from God. They may be from God. They may be from nature. They may be from the devil. Therefore, "Do not believe every spirit, but test the spirits to see whether they are from God."[5] Test all things by the written word, and let all bow down before it. You are in danger of enthusiasm every hour if you depart at all from Scripture, or from the plain, literal meaning of any text read within its context. You are in danger if you despise or disregard reason, knowledge, or human learning. Every one of these is an excellent gift of God and may serve the noblest purposes.

I advise you never to use the words *wisdom, reason,* or *knowledge* by way of rebuke. On the contrary, pray that you yourself may abound in them more and more. If you mean worldly wisdom, useless knowledge, or false reasoning, then say so. Throw away the chaff, but not the wheat.

One general entrance to enthusiasm is expecting the end without the means. For example:

- expecting knowledge without searching the Scriptures and consulting the children of God;
- expecting spiritual strength without constant prayer and steady watchfulness;
- expecting any blessing without hearing the word of God at every opportunity.

Some have been ignorant of this device of Satan. They have abandoned searching the Scriptures. They said, "God writes all the Scriptures on my heart. Therefore, I don't need to read them." Others thought they no longer needed to hear the word of God and so grew lax in attending the morning preaching services. O take warning! You have listened to the voice of a stranger. Fly back to Christ and follow in the good old way, which was "once delivered to the saints"[6] the way that even the unbelieving bore testimony "that the Christians rose early every day to sing hymns to Christ as God."

The very desire for "growing in grace" may sometimes be a door for enthusiasm to let itself into the heart. Because it constantly leads us to seek new grace, it may lead us unwittingly to seek something else new besides new measures of love of God and neighbor. Therefore, it has led some to seek and believe that they have received gifts of a new kind, after a new heart, such as

(1) loving God with all our mind
(2) loving God with all our soul
(3) loving God with all our strength
(4) oneness with God
(5) oneness with Christ
(6) having our life hid with Christ in God
(7) being dead with Christ
(8) rising with Christ
(9) sitting with Christ in heavenly places
(10) being taken up into Christ's throne
(11) being in the New Jerusalem
(12) seeing the tabernacle of God come down among the people
(13) being dead to all works
(14) not being subject to death, pain, grief, or temptation

One reason for many of these mistakes is taking every new, strong application of any of these Scriptures to heart and believing them to be a new kind of gift. Those who do so do not know that several of these Scriptures are not fulfilled yet. They do not know that most of the others are fulfilled when we are justified, and the rest are fulfilled the moment we are sanctified. It remains only to experience them in higher degrees. This is all we have to expect.

Another reason for these, and a thousand mistakes, is not considering deeply that love is the highest gift of God: humble, gentle, patient love. All visions, revelations, manifestations, whatever, are small things compared to love. All the gifts mentioned above are either the same with, or infinitely inferior to, love.

It is important that you thoroughly understand this—"the heaven of heavens is love." There is nothing higher in religion. There is, in effect, nothing else. If you look for anything but more love, you are looking wide of the mark and getting out of the royal way. And when you are asking others, "Have you received this or that blessing?" if you mean anything but more love, you mean wrong. You are leading them out of the way and putting them upon a false path. Settle it then in your heart that from the moment God has saved you from all sin you are to strive for nothing more than more of the love described in

> By faith we are come
> To our permanent home;
> By hope we the rapture improve;
> By love we still rise,
> And look down on the skies,
> For the heaven of heavens is love.
>
> *Collection*, #486, stanza 3

Abraham's bosom: See Luke 16:19-31.

antinomianism: the belief that those saved by grace are thus freed from any scriptural, civil, or moral laws and that salvation is attained solely through faith and the gift of divine grace

moral law, law of love: The **moral law** is the Law given by God through Moses. Its purpose is three-fold:

1. to convict of sin
2. to lead us to Christ
3. to keep us with Christ and help us grow in grace.

The **law of love** is described in 1 Corinthians 13 and summarized in the Great Commandment to love God with all your heart, soul, mind, and strength, and to love your neighbor as yourself. The two are, for Wesley, interrelated and inter-dependent.

cockatrice: a fabled reptile hatched by a serpent from a cock's egg and having the power to kill by its glance or breath. In Scripture, *cockatrice* refers to any venomous creature.

shibboleth: a slogan or password that sets you apart from others, making them outsiders. From Judges 12:6: "They said to him, 'Then say Shibboleth,' and he said, 'Sibboleth,' for he could not pronounce it right. Then they seized him and killed him."

1 Corinthians 13. You can go no higher than this until you are carried into **Abraham's bosom**.

I say one more time, beware of enthusiasm. It is the imagining that you have the gift of prophesying, or of discerning of spirits, which I do not believe that even one of you has or has ever had yet. Beware of judging people to be either right or wrong according to your own feelings. This is not a scriptural way of judging. Keep close to "the law and to the testimony!"[7]

Q. 34. What is the third advice you would give those who have fallen from grace?

A. Beware of **antinomianism**, or "canceling out any part of the law through faith."[8] Enthusiasm naturally leads to this. Indeed they can hardly be separated. This may creep up on you in a thousand ways. Therefore, you cannot be too alert against it. Be on your guard against everything, whether in principle or practice, that resembles it at all. Even the great truth, that "Christ is the end of the law,"[9] may betray us into antinomianism if we do not consider that he has adopted every point of the **moral law** and grafted it into the **law of love**.

Beware of thinking, "Because I am filled with love, I don't need to have so much holiness. Because I pray always, I don't need a set time for private prayer. Because I am always mindful of my behavior, I don't need personal self-examination." Let us "magnify the law," the whole written word, "and make it honorable."[10] Let this be our proclamation: "I prize your commandments above gold or precious stones. O what love I have for your law! I study in it all day long."

Beware of antinomian books. They contain many excellent things, and this makes them all the more dangerous. O be warned in time! Do not play with fire. Do not put your hand on the hole of a **cockatrice**'s den.

I beg you, beware of bigotry. Do not confine your love or generosity only to Methodists, much less to that very small part of them who seem to be renewed in love, or to those who believe yours and their testimony. Do not make this your **shibboleth**! Beware of **stillness**. It is wrong to refrain from the means of grace for false reasons. Here is one example out of many: One may say, "You have received a great blessing. But you began to talk about it and to do this and that good work. Consequently, you lost it. You should have been still."

Beware of self-indulgence. Some even make a virtue of it, laughing at self-denial and taking up the cross daily, at fasting or abstinence.

Beware of intolerance. Abstain from thinking or calling people blind, dead, fallen, or "enemies to the work" who in any way oppose you, whether in belief or practice.

Once more, beware of **solifidianism**. Refrain from crying nothing but, "Believe, believe!" and condemning those who speak in a more scriptural way as being ignorant or believing in salvation by works. At certain times, indeed, it may be all right to deal with nothing but repentance or faith, or only holiness. But in general our call is to declare the whole word of God, and to teach and preach according to the **analogy of faith**.

The written Word (Scripture) takes into account the whole of righteousness, down to the smallest detail. It does this to such an extent as to be serious, considerate, careful, patient, and giving honor to all people. So, likewise, the Holy Spirit works the same in our hearts, not merely creating the desire for holiness in general, but strongly inclining us to every particular grace, leading us to every individual part of "whatever is lovely."[11] This is of the greatest importance because "by works faith is made perfect."[12] Therefore, completing or destroying the work of faith, and enjoying the favor or suffering the displeasure of God, greatly depend on every single act of obedience or disobedience.

Q. 35. What is the fourth advice you would give those who have fallen from grace?

A. Beware of sins of omission. Do not neglect any opportunity for doing good of any kind. Be eager for good works. Do not intentionally omit any work of piety or mercy. Do all the good you possibly can to the bodies and souls of human beings. Particularly, "Warn your neighbor about sin so that you can help your neighbor overcome sin, and you yourself will not incur sin by omission." Be active. Give no place to habitual idleness. Do not say, "You are lazy, lazy."[13] Many will continue to say so, but let your whole spirit and behavior disprove their lie. Always be busy doing something productive. Lose no shred of time. "Gather up the fragments so that nothing is lost."[14] And whatever your hand finds to do, do it with all your might.

Be "slow to speak"[15] and cautious in speaking. "When words are many, transgression is not lacking."[16] Do not talk too much or for a long time. Few people can converse profitably for more than an hour. Keep a great distance from pious chitchat and religious gossiping.

Q. 36. What is the fifth advice you would give those who have fallen from grace?

A. Beware of desiring anything but God. Now you desire nothing else; every other desire is driven out. See that none enter again. "Keep yourself pure";[17] let your eye remain healthy, and "your whole body will be full of light."[18] Allow no desire of pleasing food or any other pleasure of sense. Allow no desire of pleasing the eye or the imagination by anything grand, or new, or beautiful. Allow no desire of money, praise, or esteem. Do not desire happiness in any creature. You may feel some of these desires when you try to come back into grace from your fall, but there is no reason to. You need feel them no more. Stand firm in the liberty with which Christ has made you free.

stillness: also known as quietism; the belief that the means of grace should not be practiced until one receives the assurance of faith. Stillness was encouraged by the Moravians who came to dominate the Fetter Lane Society in London. Philip Molther convinced many in the society that they lacked true faith and encouraged them to remain "still" before the Lord. He believed that Christ was the only means of grace, and that until people had true faith they should refrain from other means, especially the Lord's Supper.

solifidianism: the belief that salvation is by faith alone to the exclusion of good works

analogy of faith: understanding God's Word as a whole rather than through individual or obscure passages

Wesley on faith:
"'But what is that faith by which we are sanctified, saved from sin, and perfected in love?'
1. Faith is a divine evidence and conviction that God has promised perfection in love in the Holy Scripture. . . .
2. Faith is a divine evidence and conviction that what God has promised he is *able* to do . . .
3. Faith is a divine evidence and conviction that God is able and willing to do it *now* . . .

To this confidence, that God is both able and willing to sanctify us *now*, one more thing needs to be added: a divine evidence and conviction that *he does it*."

From Sermon 43, "The Scripture Way of Salvation," in *The Works of John Wesley.*

> Jesu, the word of mercy give,
>   And let it swiftly run;
> And let the priests themselves believe,
>   And put salvation on.
>
> Clothed with the spirit of holiness,
>   May all thy people prove
> The plenitude of gospel grace,
>   The joy of perfect love.
>
> *Collection*, #434, stanzas 1–2

society, class, band: the organizing structures of the Methodist movement.

The **society** was the large group, comparable to today's local church. It served as a place where Christians could strengthen one another's faith, be accountable to one another, and be mutually responsible for one another.

When the several societies became too large and geographically spread out to carry out the above purposes, they were divided into smaller groups known as **classes**. Every Methodist was expected to attend his or her class meeting every week. The purpose of the class meeting was support and accountability for Christian faith and life.

The **band** was a still smaller group, segregated by gender and marital status. There the nature of accountability was deeper and more intimate. While everyone was required to meet with a class, the band was an option for those who sought a deeper discipleship.

Be patterns to all of denying yourselves and taking up your cross daily.[19] Let them see that you disregard any pleasure that does not bring you nearer to God, and any pain that does, and that you simply aim at pleasing God, whether by doing or suffering. Let them see that the constant language of your heart, with regard to pleasure or pain, honor or dishonor, riches or poverty, is,

> All's alike to me, so I
> In my Lord may live and die!

Q. 37. What is the sixth advice you would give those who have fallen from grace?

A. Beware of schism or causing separation within the church of Christ. Such internal division begins when sisters and brothers in Christ, the members of his body, no longer have love "for one another" (1 Corinthians 12:25, NRSV). This is the beginning of all conflict that ultimately leads to every outward separation. Beware of everything that contributes to such discord.

Beware of a dividing spirit. Avoid whatever resembles it in any way. Therefore, do not say, "I belong to Paul," or, "I belong to Apollos" (1 Corinthians 3:4, NRSV). That is what caused the divisions Paul faced at Corinth. Do not say, "This is my preacher, the best preacher in England. Give me him and take all the rest." All this tends to encourage division and disunite those whom God has brought together. Do not despise or put down any preacher. Do not exalt any one above the rest. This will only hurt both the preacher and the cause of God. On the other hand, be forgiving and patient with those preachers who may not always express themselves clearly or who make the occasional mistake in judgment.

Likewise, if you would avoid schism, observe every rule of the <u>society</u> and the bands for conscience' sake. Never skip meeting your <u>class</u> or <u>band</u>. Never absent yourself from any public meeting. These are the very fabric of our society. Whatever weakens, or tends to weaken, our regard for these or our diligence in attending them strikes at the very heart of our community. As one said, "That part of our community, the private weekly meetings for prayer, examination, and instruction, has been the greatest means of deepening and confirming every blessing that was received by the word preached and of spreading it to others who could not attend the public ministry. Without this religious connection and fellowship, the most ardent attempts by mere preaching have proved of no lasting use."

Do not tolerate any thought of separating from your brothers and sisters, whether their opinions agree with yours or not. Do not dream that anyone sins because he or she doesn't believe you or take your word, or that this or that opinion is essential to the work, and both must stand or fall together.

Beware of being impatient with those who contradict you. Do not condemn or think harshly of those who cannot see just as you see or who believe that they must contradict you, whether in a large matter or a small one. I fear that some of us have thought harshly of others merely because they contradicted what we affirmed. Such thoughts lead to division; and by doing things of this kind, we are teaching them an evil lesson against ourselves.

Do not be thin-skinned, irritable, or combative. Refrain from arguing with those who do not implicitly accept my teachings or the teachings of other Methodist leaders.

Expect contradiction and opposition, together with crosses of various kinds. Consider the words of Saint Paul: "For he [God] has graciously granted you the privilege," for Christ's sake, as a fruit of his death and intercession for you, "not only of believing in Christ, but of suffering for him as well" (Philippians 1:29, NRSV). *It is given!* God gives you this opposition or criticism. It is a fresh token of God's love. Will you disown the Giver or reject the gift and consider it a misfortune? Will you not rather say, "Father, the hour is come that you should be glorified. Now you give your child to suffer something for you. Do with me according to your will"?[20]

You need to know that these things, far from being blockages to the work of God or to your soul, unless by your own fault, are not only unavoidable in the course of God's divine care and guardianship but useful and necessary for you. Therefore, receive them from God (not from chance) with willingness and thankfulness. Receive them from others with humility, meekness, gentleness, and sweetness. Why shouldn't even your outward appearance and manner be pleasant?

Beware of tempting others to separate from you. Commit no offense that can possibly be avoided. Make sure that you practice what you preach, glorifying the doctrine of God our Savior. Be particularly careful in speaking of yourself. Do not deny the work of God; but when you are called upon, speak of it in the most inoffensive manner possible. Avoid all magnificent, pompous words. Indeed, you need not give the work of God in your life any general name, such as *perfection, sanctification,* the *second blessing,* nor *the attainment* of it. Rather speak of your own experience of what God has done for you. You may say, "At such a time I felt a change that I am not able to express, and since that time I have not felt pride, or self-will, or anger, or unbelief, or anything but a fullness of love for God and for all humankind." Answer any other plain question that is asked with modesty and simplicity.

If any of you should at any time fall from perfection in love, if you should again feel pride or unbelief or any habitual sin from which you are now delivered, at the peril of your soul do not deny, hide, or disguise it at all. In such a time, go to one in whom you can confide and speak exactly what you feel. God will enable him or her

As giants may they run their race,
  Exulting in their might,
As burning luminaries chase
  The gloom of hellish night.

As the great Sun of Righteousness
  Their healing wings display,
And let their lustre still increase
  Unto the perfect day.

Collection, #434, stanzas 5–6

to speak a word of grace that shall be health to your soul. Certainly God will again lift up your head and cause the bones that have been broken to rejoice.[21]

Q. 38. What is the last advice that you would give those who have fallen from grace?

A. Be exemplary in all things, particularly in outward things (as in dress), in little things, in the use of your money (avoiding every needless expense), in deep, steady earnestness, and in the consistency and usefulness of all your life in the world. You shall be "a light shining in a dark place."[22] You shall daily "grow in grace,"[23] until "entry into the eternal kingdom of our Lord and Savior Jesus Christ will be richly provided for you."[24]

Endnotes

1. See 1 Corinthians 12:14-26.
2. 1 Thessalonians 5:12, NRSV
3. Philippians 2:5
4. 1 Peter 5:5, NRSV
5. 1 John 4:1, NRSV
6. Jude 1:3
7. Isaiah 8:19-20
8. Romans 3:31
9. Romans 10:4
10. Isaiah 42:21
11. Philippians 4:8
12. James 2:22
13. Exodus 5:17, NRSV
14. John 6:12
15. James 1:19
16. Proverbs 10:19, NRSV
17. 1 Timothy 5:22
18. Matthew 6:22
19. See Luke 9:23.
20. See John 17:1-2.
21. See Psalm 51:8.
22. 2 Peter 1:19
23. 2 Peter 3:18
24. 2 Peter 1:11, NRSV

VIII

Most of the preceding advice is supported in the following reflections, which, next to the holy Scriptures, I commend to your deep and frequent consideration:

(1) The sea is an excellent image of the fullness of God and of the blessed Spirit. For as the rivers all return to the sea, so the bodies, souls, and good works of the righteous return to God, to live there in God's eternal home.

Although all the graces of God depend on God's abundance, God is generally pleased to attach them to the prayers, the teaching, and the holiness of those whom God gives to be our examples in faith. By strong though invisible attractions, God draws some souls through their relationships with others.

The kinships formed by grace far surpass those formed by nature.

The truly devout show that passions flow just as naturally from true as from false love. They are deeply aware of the goods and evils of those whom they love for God's sake. But only those who understand the language of love can comprehend this.

The depth of the soul may be calm, even while we are in many outward troubles. In the same way, the bottom of the sea is calm while the surface is in turmoil.

The best helps to growth in grace are the abuses, the insults, and the losses that come our way. We should receive them with all thankfulness. We prefer them to all others because they are not our doing. They come upon us only as a consequence of our striving to follow Christ in the world.

The quickest way to escape from our sufferings is to want them to endure as long as God pleases.

Suffering persecution and affliction in a righteous manner on a single occasion does more to conform us to the image of Christ than we could have done by merely imitating his mercy in many good works.

One of the greatest evidences of God's love for those that love God is to send them afflictions along with grace to bear them. Even in the greatest afflictions, we need to testify to God that in receiving them from God's hand, we feel pleasure in the midst of the pain from being afflicted by God, who loves us and whom we love.

The most direct way God uses to draw us to God is to afflict us in the thing we love most, and with good reason. God will cause this affliction to arise from some good action done on behalf of the object of our love. The effect is to reveal to us the true emptiness of what the world regards as lovely and desirable.

(2) True surrender is a complete conformity to the whole will of God, who wills and does all (except sin) that comes to pass in the world. In order to do this, we have only to embrace all events, good and bad, as God's will.

In the greatest misfortunes that may happen to the righteous, either from heaven or earth, they remain steadfast in peace and perfectly submissive to God. They are able to do this by an inward, loving regard for God, uniting in one all the powers of their souls.

We ought to quietly suffer whatever befalls us, to bear the faults of others and our own, to confess them to God in secret prayer or with groans that are too deep to be spoken in words.[1] But we must never speak a sharp or disagreeable word, nor murmur or sigh. Be thoroughly willing that God should treat you in the manner that is pleasing to God. After all, we are God's lambs and, therefore, ought to be ready to suffer, even to the death, without complaining.

We are to bear with those we cannot change and be content with offering them to God. This is true surrender. Because Christ has borne our infirmities,[2] we may well bear those of one another for Christ's sake.

To abandon everything, to strip one's self bare in order to seek and to follow Jesus Christ naked to Bethlehem where he was born, naked to the hall where he was scourged, and naked to Calvary where he died on the cross is so great a mercy that both the will to do it and the knowledge of it is given to anyone only through faith in the Son of God.

(3) There is no love of God without patience, and no patience without humility and sweetness of spirit.

Humility and patience are the surest proofs of the increase of love.

Humility alone unites patience with love, without which it is impossible to draw any benefit from suffering, or indeed, to avoid complaint. This is especially true when we think we have given no cause for suffering we endure at the hands of others.

True humility is a kind of denial of self.[3] This is the center of all virtues.

A soul returned to God ought to pay close attention to everything that is said to him or her about salvation, with a desire to grow in holiness of heart and life.

Of the sins God has forgiven, let nothing remain but a deeper humility in the heart and a more disciplined ordering of our words, our actions, and our sufferings.

(4) Tolerating others and suffering evils in meekness and silence is the sum of a Christian life.

82

God is the first object of our love. Love's next responsibility is to bear the failings of others. And we should begin the practice of this amidst our own household.

We should especially practice our love toward those who most shock either our way of thinking, our temperament, our knowledge, or the desire we have that others should be as virtuous as we wish to be ourselves.

(5) God rarely gives his Spirit, even to those who have been established in grace, if they do not pray for it on all occasions, not only once but many times.

God does nothing but in answer to prayer. Even the people who have been converted to God without praying for it themselves (which is extremely rare) were prayed for by others. Every new victory that a soul gains is the effect of a new prayer.

Whenever we experience anxiety, we should steep ourselves in prayer. In those times, we need to open our hearts and minds to the grace and light of God. Only then will we be prepared to make decisions in accord with God's will, without concern for any success or failure they may bring.

In the greatest temptations a single look to Christ and simply speaking his name is enough to overcome the wicked one. Let it be done with confidence and calmness of spirit.

God's command to "pray without ceasing"[4] is founded on the need we have of grace to sustain the life of God in the soul. This life God gives can no more survive one moment without God's grace than the body can without air.

When we think of or speak to God, whether we act or suffer for God, all is prayer when we have no other goal than God's love and the desire to please God.

All that a Christian does, even in eating and sleeping, is prayer when it is done in simplicity, according to the command of God, without either adding to or diminishing from it by personal choice.

Prayer continues in the desire of the heart, though the understanding is worked out in outward actions.

In souls filled with love, the desire to please God is a ceaseless prayer.

We call the furious hate that the devil bears us "the roaring of a lion"; we may likewise call our vehement love "crying after God."

All God requires of God's adult children is that their hearts be truly purified, and that they continually offer to God the desires and promises that naturally flow from perfect love. These desires, being the genuine fruits of love,[5] are the most perfect prayers that can flow from such love.

(6) It is difficult to comprehend how narrow the way of life is into which God leads those who would follow.[6] It is equally difficult to understand how dependent upon God we must be; that is, unless we are lacking in faithfulness to God.

church, house: This section, beginning on page 81 with "(1) The sea is an excellent image . . . ," is an extended quotation from *Instructions chrestiennes*, by Jean Duvergier de Hauranne (1581–1643), also known as Saint-Cyran. Hauranne is saying that we should take our piety home with us from church.

It is difficult for many to believe the great significance God places upon the smallest of things. It is also hard for many to grasp the many troubles that sometimes flow from those faults that appear to be minor failings.

A small speck of dust will cause a clock to malfunction, and a single grain of sand will obscure our sight. Likewise, a single grain of sin in the heart will hinder its right motion toward God.

We ought to be in the **church** as the saints are in heaven, and in the **house** as the holiest people are in the church, doing our work in the house as we pray in the church, worshiping God from the depths of the heart.

We should be continually working to cut off all the useless things that surround us. God usually decreases the excesses of our souls in the same proportion as we do those of our bodies.

The best means of resisting the devil is to destroy whatever of the world remains in us in order to raise for God, upon its ruins, a building all of love. Then we shall begin, in this short life, to love God now as we will love in eternity.

We rarely realize how easy it is to rob God of his due in our friendship with the most virtuous people, until they are torn from us by death. But if this loss produces lasting sorrow, that is a clear proof that we had two treasures between which we divided our heart.

(7) After we have renounced all sin, we must be constantly on guard against temptation if we are to remain free. We need to pray for God's vigilance to supplement ours. Failing to watch and pray will lead us to once again be captured and overcome.

Just as dangerous winds may enter a house through tiny openings, the devil never enters more dangerously than by small, unnoticed events that seem to be insignificant. Yet they gradually open the heart to great temptations.

It is good to renew ourselves from time to time by thorough self-examination of the state of our soul as if we have never examined it before. Nothing contributes more to the full assurance of faith than keeping ourselves in humility and the exercise of all good works.

Add to constant watchfulness and prayer steady employment. For grace fills a vacuum as well as nature, and the devil fills whatever God does not fill.

There is no faithfulness like that which should exist between a guide of souls and the person directed by him or her. The guide and the one guided must regularly honor each other in God and closely examine themselves to assure that all their thoughts are pure and all their words directed with Christian judgment. Other affairs are only the things of humans, but these are singularly the things of God.

(8) The words of Saint Paul, "No one can say 'Jesus is Lord' except by the Holy Spirit,"[7] show us the necessity of looking to God in our good works and even in our smallest thoughts. We know that only those that God forms in

us and with us are pleasing to God. Consequently, we learn that we cannot serve God unless our tongue, hands, and heart are used by God and the Spirit to do what God would have us do.

If we were not utterly impotent, our good works would be our own property. But now they belong entirely to God because they flow from God and from God's grace. While giving rise to our works and making them sanctified, God is honored in us through them.

One of the cardinal rules of religion is to lose no opportunity to serve God. Because God cannot be seen, we are to serve God in our neighbor. God receives such service as if it were done to God in person, standing visibly before us.[8]

God does not love people who are inconsistent, or good works that are sporadic. The only thing pleasing to God is a life and service that resembles God's own constancy and faithfulness.

A constant attention to the work that God entrusts to us is a mark of solid piety.

Love fasts when it can and as much as it can. It leads to all the means of grace and applies itself in all the outward works it is able to do. It flies, as it were, like Elijah over the plain to find God upon his holy mountain.[9]

God is so great that greatness is given to the smallest thing that is done for God's service.

Happy are they who are sick or even lose their life for doing a good work.

God frequently conceals the part that we children have in the conversion of other souls. However, whenever a soul is converted to God, we may boldly say that one of the chief causes is the person who persistently intercedes before God for that conversion.

Charity cannot be practiced correctly unless
- first, we perform it the moment God gives the opportunity, and
- second, we depart immediately afterward to offer it to God in humble thanksgiving. We do this for three reasons:
  1. to return to God what we have received from God;
  2. to avoid the dangerous temptation that emerges from the very goodness of these works;
  3. to unite ourselves to God, in whom the soul expands itself in prayer, with all the graces we have received and the good works we have done, to draw from God new strength against the bad effects these very works may produce in us if we do not make use of the antidotes God has ordained against these poisons.

The true way to be filled anew with the riches of grace is to strip ourselves of it. Without this it is extremely difficult not to grow faint in the practice of good works.

Good works are not complete in their own right until they lose themselves in God. This is a kind of death to them. It

O that in me the sacred fire
  Might now begin to glow,
Burn up the dross of base desire,
  And make the mountains flow!

O that it now from heaven might fall,
  And all my sins consume!
Come, Holy Ghost, for thee I call,
  Spirit of burning, come!

Refining fire, go through my heart,
  Illuminate my soul;
Scatter thy life through every part,
  And sanctify the whole.

Collection, #351, stanzas 7–9

Hebrews 6:1:

"Therefore let us go on toward perfection, leaving behind the basic teaching about Christ, and not laying again the foundation: repentance from dead works and faith toward God."

Philippians 3:15:

"Let those of us then who are mature [perfect] be of the same mind; and if you think differently about anything, this too God will reveal to you."

1 John 4:18:

"There is no fear in love, but perfect love casts out fear; for fear has to do with punishment, and whoever fears has not reached perfection in love."

1 Thessalonians 5:16-18:

"Rejoice always, pray without ceasing, give thanks in all circumstances; for this is the will of God in Christ Jesus for you."

resembles the death of our bodies. For it is only in death that the body, losing itself in the glory of God, shall attain immortality. In this spiritual death, good works are stripped only of all earthly and mortal pride.

Fire is the symbol of love. The love of God is the beginning and the end of all our good works. But truth surpasses symbol. The fire of divine love has this advantage over material fire: it can return to its source and raise with it all the good works that it produces. In so doing it prevents corruption by pride, vanity, or any evil mixture. This can be done only when these good works have their beginning and their end in God. This is done through deep gratitude that plunges the soul into God as into an abyss. All that it is and all the grace and works for which it is indebted to God must be returned to God. This is a gratitude through which the soul seems to empty itself of good works so that they may return to their source, like rivers seem willing to empty themselves when they pour themselves into the sea.

When we have received any blessing from God, we need to withdraw, if not into our prayer closets then into our hearts, and say, "I come, Lord, to restore to you what you have given. I freely relinquish it, to enter again into my own insignificance. For what is the most perfect creature in heaven or earth in your presence but an empty vessel capable of being filled with you and by you? It is like the air that is empty and dark and capable of being filled with the light of the sun that withdraws every day and returns the next. There is nothing in the air that either possesses this light or resists it. O give me the same ease of receiving and restoring your grace and good works! I say *your* grace and good works, O God, for I acknowledge the source from which thy spring is in you, and not in me."

26. In the year 1764, upon a review of the whole subject, I wrote down a summary of what I had observed in the following short suppositions:

(1) There is such a thing as perfection, for it is mentioned again and again in Scripture.
(2) It does not precede justification, for justified people are to "go on toward perfection" (Hebrews 6:1).
(3) It is not reserved for the time of death, for Saint Paul speaks of living people who were perfect (Philippians 3:15).
(4) It is not absolute. Absolute perfection does not belong to human beings, nor to angels, but to God alone.
(5) It does not make a person infallible. No one is infallible while he or she remains in the body.
(6) Is it sinless? It is not worth the effort to argue. Perfection, as understood here, is salvation from sin.
(7) It is "perfect love" (1 John 4:18). This is the essence of it. Its properties, or inseparable fruits, are rejoicing always, praying without ceasing, and giving thanks in all circumstances (1 Thessalonians 5:16-18).

(8) It grows and matures. It is so far from being incapable of increase that one perfected in love may grow in grace far swifter than before.

(9) It is capable of being lost. We have numerous examples of this, but we were not thoroughly convinced of this until five or six years ago.

(10) It is constantly both preceded and followed by a gradual work.

(11) But is it in itself instantaneous or not? In examining this, let us go on step by step.

An instantaneous change occurred in some believers. No one can deny this. Since that change, they have enjoyed perfect love. They feel this and this alone. They "rejoice always, pray without ceasing, and give thanks in everything."[10] Now, this is all that I mean by perfection. Therefore, these believers are witnesses of the perfection that I preach.

"But in some this change was not instantaneous." They did not perceive the instant when it happened. It is often difficult to perceive the instant when a person dies; yet there is an instant in which life ceases. And if ever sin ceases, there must be a last moment of its existence and a first moment of our deliverance from it.

"But if they have this love now, they will lose it." They may; but they need not. And whether they do or not, they have it now. They experience now what we teach. They now are all love. They now rejoice, pray, and praise without ceasing.

"However, sin is only suspended in them; it is not destroyed." Call it what you please. They are all love today and they take no thought for tomorrow.

"But this doctrine has been much abused." So has that of justification by faith. But that is no reason for giving up either this or any other scriptural doctrine. "When you wash your child," as one says, "throw away the water, but do not throw away the child."

"But those who think they are saved from sin say they have no need of the merits of Christ." They say exactly the opposite. Their language is,

> Every moment, Lord, I want
> The merit of thy death!

They never before had so deep, so unspeakable, a conviction of the need of **Christ in all his offices** as they have now.

Therefore, all our preachers should make a point of preaching perfection to believers constantly, strongly, and explicitly. All believers should mind this one thing and continually agonize for it.

27. I have now done what I proposed. I have given a plain and simple account of the manner in which I first received the doctrine of

Christ in all his offices: Wesley believed that Christ's death and resurrection were the culmination of his past ministry. He went on to say that Christ in all of his offices is the foundation of his present work. Wesley frequently taught that Christ must be preached in the three offices of Priest, Prophet, and King/Physician:

• **Christ the Priest** offers forgiveness of sins. He restores us to relationship with God and, through continual pardon, helps us stay in relationship with God. Christians never outgrow their need for Christ in this office.

• **Christ the Prophet** overcomes the power of sin for his people. He restores to us knowledge of God's will for human life through the revelation of God's law (see the Sermon on the Mount, Matthew 5–7).

• **Christ the King** guides Christians on their way to holiness of heart and life. As they follow and obey his commands, they are restored to wholeness and perfected in love.

See Sermon 36, "The Law Established Through Faith, Discourse II," in *The Works of John Wesley*, including the following:

"We are not ourselves clear before God unless we proclaim Christ in all his offices. To preach Christ as a worker that need not be ashamed is to preach him not only as our great 'High Priest—taken from among humans and ordained for humans in things pertaining to God,' as such 'reconciling us to God by his blood' and 'always living to make intercession for us'—but also as the Prophet of the Lord, 'who became for us wisdom from God,' who by his word and his Spirit 'is with us always,' 'guiding us into all truth.' And indeed he is remaining a King forever, giving laws to all whom he has bought with his blood, restoring those to the image of God whom he had first reinstated in his favor, reigning in all believing hearts until he has 'subdued all things to himself,' until he has completely cast out all sin, and 'brought in everlasting righteousness.'"

perfection. I have also explained the sense in which I received, continue to receive, and teach it to this day. I have explained what I mean by that scriptural expression, both in whole and every part of it. I have drawn the full picture of it, without either disguise or covering.

I would now ask any impartial person, What is so frightful about this teaching? From where is all this outcry, which for these twenty years and more has been made throughout the kingdom as if all Christianity were destroyed and all religion torn up by the roots? Why is it that the very name of perfection has been cast out of the mouths of Christians, indeed, discredited and detestable as if it contained the most evil heresy? Why have the preachers of it been hooted at like mad dogs, even by those who fear God, and even by some of their own fellow Methodists, some whom they, under God, had helped become believers through the gospel? What reason is there for this, or what pretense? There is no sound reason. It is impossible that there could be.

But there are falsehoods in great abundance. Indeed, there is ground to fear that, with some who treat us in this way, it is simple dishonesty—no more than a false appearance from the beginning to the end. They wanted and sought opportunity against me, and here they found what they sought. "This is Mr. Wesley's doctrine! He preaches perfection!" I do. Yet this is not my doctrine any more than it is yours, or anyone else's that is a minister of Christ. For it is God's doctrine—peculiarly, emphatically God's. It is the doctrine of Jesus Christ. Those are his words, not mine: "Be perfect, therefore, as your heavenly Father is perfect."[11]

Who says you shall not be perfect, or at least not until your soul is separated from the body? Perfection is the doctrine of Saint Paul, the doctrine of Saint James, of Saint Peter, and Saint John. It is not Mr. Wesley's any more than it is the doctrine of everyone who preaches the pure and the whole gospel.

I tell you as plain as I can speak where and when I found this. I found it in the word of God, in the Old and New Testaments, when I read them with no other intent or desire but to save my own soul.

But whoever this doctrine belongs to, I pray you, what harm is there in it? Look at it again. Examine it closely on every side. In one view, it is purity of intention, dedicating all the life to God. It is giving God all our heart. It is one desire and intent ruling all our habits and attitudes. It is devoting not only a part but all of our soul, body, and wealth to God. In another aspect, it is all the mind that was in Christ, enabling us to walk as Christ walked. It is the circumcision of the heart from all impurity, all inward as well as outward pollution. It is a renewal of the heart in the whole image of God, the full likeness of the One who created it. In yet another, it is loving God with all our heart, and our neighbor as ourselves.

Now, take it in any of these views you please (for there is no material difference), and this is the whole of perfection, as a succession of writings prove, that I have believed and taught for these forty years, from 1725 to 1765.

28. Now let this perfection appear in its original form. Who can speak one word against it? Will any dare to speak against loving the Lord our God with all our heart, and our neighbor as ourselves? Can anyone be against a renewal of heart, not only in part but in the whole image of God? Who will open his or her mouth against being cleansed from all pollution both of flesh and spirit? Who is against having all the mind that was in Christ, and walking in all things as Christ walked? What person who calls himself or herself a Christian has the audacity to object to devoting not a part but all of our soul, body, and substance to God? What serious person would oppose giving God all our heart and having one aim ruling all our habits and attitudes?

I say again, let this perfection appear in its own shape, and who will fight against it? It must be disguised before it can be opposed. It must be covered with a bear skin first, or even the wild beasts of the people will hardly be persuaded to worry with it.

But whatever those who may be opposed do, let not the children of God fight any longer against the image of God. Let not the members of Christ say anything against having the whole mind that was in Christ. Let not those who are alive to God oppose dedicating all our life to God.

Why should you who have God's love filling your heart withstand the giving him all your heart? Does not all that is within you cry out, "O who that loves can love enough?" What pity that those who desire and aim to please God should have any other aim or desire! It is even more a pity that they should dread as a fatal delusion, indeed abhor as an abomination to God, having this one desire and design ruling every habit and thought! Why should devout people be afraid of devoting all their soul, body, and substance to God? Why should those who love Christ count it a damnable error to think we may have all the mind that was in him?

We allow, we contend, that we are justified freely through the righteousness and the blood of Christ. Why are you so hot against us because we expect likewise to be sanctified wholly through his Spirit?

We look for no favor either from the open servants of sin or from those who have only the form of religion. But how long will you who worship God in spirit, who are "circumcised with the circumcision not made with hands,"[12] fight against those who seek an entire circumcision of heart, who thirst to be cleansed "from all filthiness of flesh and spirit" and to "perfect holiness in the fear of God?"[13]

Are we your enemies because we look for a full deliverance from that "carnal mind which is hostility against God?"[14] No, we are your family, your fellow laborers in the vineyard of our Lord, your companions in the kingdom and patience of Jesus. Although this we confess (if we are fools for Christ, yet as fools bear with us), we do expect to love God with all our heart, and our neighbor as ourselves. Indeed, we do believe that God will, in this world, so **"cleanse the thoughts of our hearts, by the inspiration of the Holy Spirit, that we shall perfectly love God, and worthily magnify God's holy name."**

"cleanse the thoughts . . .":
This is a reference to the "Collect for Purity" from the weekly eucharist liturgy of the *Book of Common Prayer*. See sidebar on page 23.

Endnotes

1. See Romans 8:26-27.
2. Isaiah 53:4, NRSV
3. See Matthew 16:24-26.
4. 1 Thessalonians 5:17
5. See Galatians 5:22-23.
6. See Matthew 7:13-14.
7. 1 Corinthians 12:3, NRSV
8. See Matthew 25:40.
9. See 1 Kings 19:4-18.
10. 1 Thessalonians 5:16-18
11. Matthew 5:48, NRSV
12. Colossians 2:11
13. 2 Corinthians 7:1
14. Romans 8:7

Brief Thoughts on Christian Perfection

Some thoughts came to my mind this morning concerning Christian perfection and the manner and time of receiving it, and I believe it may be useful to write them down.

1. By perfection I mean the humble, gentle, patient love of God and our neighbor, ruling our habits, attitudes, words, and actions.

   I do not include an impossibility of falling from it, either in part or in whole. Therefore, I retract several expressions in our hymns that partly express, partly imply, such an impossibility.

   And I do not fight for the use of the term *sinless*, though I do not object against it.

2. As to the manner, I believe that this perfection is always accomplished in the soul by a simple act of faith, consequently in an instant.

   But I believe a gradual work both precedes and follows that instant.

3. As to the time, I believe that this instant of perfection is generally the instant of death, the moment before the soul leaves the body. But I believe that it may be ten, twenty, or forty years before.

   I believe that it is usually many years after justification; however, perfection may be within five years or five months after justification. I know of no conclusive argument to the contrary.

   If it must be many years after justification, I would be glad to know how many. *Pretium quotus arroget annus?* (How many years give sanction to our lines?)

   And how many days or months, or even years, can anyone allow to be between perfection and death? How far from justification must it be and how near to death?

   London, January 27, 1767

For Further Reading

John Wesley

Eight Life-Enriching Practices of United Methodists, by Henry H. Knight (Abingdon Press, 2001).

John Wesley's Sermons: An Anthology, edited by Albert C. Outler and Richard P. Heitzenrater (Abingdon Press, 1991).

Methodist Doctrine: The Essentials, by Ted Campbell (Abingdon Press, 1999).

Praying in the Wesleyan Spirit: 52 Sermons for Today, by Paul Wesley Chilcote (Upper Room Books, 2001).

Responsible Grace: John Wesley's Practical Theology, by Randy L. Maddox (Abingdon Press, 1994).

Rethinking Wesley's Theology for Contemporary Methodism, edited by Randy L. Maddox (Abingdon Press, 1998).

The New Creation: John Wesley's Theology Today, by Theodore Runyon (Abingdon Press, 1998).

The Wesleyan Tradition: A Paradigm for Renewal, edited by Paul W. Chilcote (Abingdon Press, 2002).

Wesley and Sanctification, by Harald Lindström (Zondervan Corporation, 1980).

Wesley and the People Called Methodists, by Richard P. Heitzenrater (Abingdon Press, 1995).

Covenant Discipleship

Accountable Discipleship: Living in God's Household, by Steven W. Manskar (Discipleship Resources, 2000).

Guide for Class Leaders: A Model for Christian Formation, by Grace Bradford (Discipleship Resources, 1999).

Guide for Covenant Discipleship Groups, by Gayle Turner Watson (Discipleship Resources, 2000).

Sprouts: Covenant Discipleship With Children, by Edie Genung Harris and Shirley L. Ramsey (Discipleship Resources, 2002).

Together in Love: Covenant Discipleship With Youth, by David C. Sutherland (Discipleship Resources, 1999).

Study Guide

by Diana L. Hynson

This "plain account" by John Wesley was intended for those "who desire to know all 'the truth as it is in Jesus.'" Wesley's hope was that this account would inspire and convict people to lead a life intimately intertwined with Jesus Christ.

During Each Study Session

• **Inquire and Pray.** Begin each time together by inquiring in love about how participants are doing—personally, vocationally, and in their relationship with God. Take time to pray at the beginning and conclusion of each session to keep the power of the Holy Spirit to transform lives at the center of your consideration of Wesley's account.

• **Sing Together.** Charles Wesley contributed thousands of hymns to the service of God's people. Use the index of your hymnal to find and either sing or say some of those hymns (or others of your choosing) in your devotional time. On occasion, a hymn text will be a part of the study text.

• **Choose Activities.** This treatise by John Wesley was written as a seamless account, but for the convenience of study it is divided into sections. Choose from among the following questions and activities to study and reflect on Wesley's text, section by section. As you go, notice references to Marjorie Suchocki's theological reflection on John Wesley's book, beginning on page 101. Think about the list of John Wesley's "Operating Principles," on page 5, which will be helpful in explaining Wesley's thought and vocabulary.

Section I

The general theme of the first section is to present the theological boundaries of what perfection is and what it is not.

A. Describe Decisions and Intentions. Review paragraphs (¶¶) 1–4, on page 11. How would you describe Wesley's decision for Christ? How would you describe his "purity of intention" regarding his "tempers"? How does this purity of intention conform to or differ from your own intentions of faith? Note the questions Wesley asks after ¶ 2 and ¶ 4. What is your personal response? Why do you think and feel as you do?

B. Study Scriptures on Holiness. Review ¶¶ 5 and 6, on pages 12–13. Individually or in teams, consider the related Scriptures (see the endnotes). Read enough of the passages to get a sense of the whole. Discuss how these passages describe for you what it means to be holy, to be perfect as God is perfect, and to have the mind that was in Christ.

For further examination, see "That Pesky Word *Perfection*" in Chapter 2 of Suchocki's theological reflection, pages 116–117.

C. Examine God's Claims. Read ¶ 10, on pages 15–17, an excerpt from *The Character of a Methodist*. Have each person look up two or three of the brief Scripture references. We relate to God in many ways. Identify what this excerpt says about God and God's claim on you
• as you think about your beliefs;
• as you hold God's love in your heart;
• as you reflect on God's vastness and eternal goodness;
• as you see God at work through church and society as an agent for justice and change.

How does the Scripture nurture and convict you to be a "perfect Christian"? By what fruits are you known? How do you love your neighbor? In what ways are your power, strength, and talents employed according to God's will?

D. Debate "Perfection on Earth." Review ¶ 11, on pages 17–18. In two teams debate whether you think there is "perfection on earth." What is the theological and biblical basis, so far, for your position?

E. Study "Imperfection." Study ¶ 12, on pages 18–21. Review "(1) In what sense Christians are not perfect." Be sure that you understand Wesley's understanding of perfection in this sense.

See also the first four paragraphs under "What Christian Perfection Is Not," in Chapter 2 of Suchocki's theological reflection, page 117.

F. Distinguish Between "Sin" and "Sins." Review the lengthy argument in (2) on the ways Christians are perfect (pages 18–21) and note Wesley's "Operating Principle #2," on page 5. First examine the distinction between sin (alienation and separation from God) and sins (the "garden variety" transgressions inherent in an imperfect world) and what the "privileges of Christians" means (see the sidebars). Skim through this section to identify the points in which Scripture indicates the presence of sins (transgressions, mistakes). Then note how Wesley counters with passages indicating how the action of God's grace through the gift of Jesus Christ has perfected humans in love by cleansing us from all sin.

Read 1 John 1:1–2:6, in which the author explains that those who accept the gracious love and gift of the Savior and abide daily in that love are brought into a righteous relationship with God ("made perfect"). What would it take for you to live daily so immersed in God's love and will for you that you would be "perfect"? Is this something that you want? Do you believe that it is attainable for yourself? for others? Why or why not?

G. Sing About the Perfected Life. Sing or say together "Love Divine, All Loves Excelling" (*The United Methodist Hymnal*, 384). How does this hymn explain or extol the perfected life?

Section II

The general theme of Section II concerns how prevenient, justifying, and sanctifying grace lead to Christian perfection.

H. Pray Together. Pray together the words of the hymn in ¶ 14, on pages 25–26, as a devotional introduction to this section.

I. Look for the "Image of God." Divide into several small groups, or work individually, and examine the various claims of the perfected life, in which the "image of God" is "stamped afresh upon our hearts" (see ¶ 13). Look up the Scripture references that support each claim, for example:
- "God has laid the axe . . . purifying their hearts" (Luke 3:9; Acts 15:9);
- They "go on from strength to strength . . . being

transformed . . . by the Lord" (Psalm 84:7; 2 Corinthians 3:18);
- Their "competence is from God" (2 Corinthians 3:5);
- Their souls are even and calm; peaceful beyond understanding (Philippians 4:7);
- They can withstand trials and suffering (1 Peter 1:6-7);
- The "love of God is poured into their hearts" (Romans 5:5).

After a time of study and discussion, spend ten to fifteen minutes in introspection, either privately or in teams of two or three. Consider the following activities to focus that time and reflect on how you feel and what you think:
- Write a journal entry or personal testimony about aligning your life to God's perfect will.
- Pray about this alignment with a partner, and lay hands on the person being prayed for.
- Either with quiet music or in silence, envision what a perfected world would be.
- Write out an action plan for matching your own sense of God's will with a social ministry that needs your particular gifts, or a plan for improving such a relationship.
- Develop a timeline using touch points in your own life when God was urging you closer to the divine will and purpose.

J. Examine Grace and Renewal. Identify the process that Wesley outlined for the "renewal of believers." (See the last part of ¶ 13, "Now, this is not to condemn those who are not renewed in love . . . ," starting on page 24, fifth paragraph.) Where do you see prevenient grace (God's preparation of the individual), justifying grace (God's action for redemption and renewal), and sanctifying grace (God's sustaining actions toward one's holiness)? How would you explain in your own words this process of God's renewal? Where have you seen God at work in your own life as you have been "assaulted again by some . . . old enemies"? What are those enemies, and what Scriptures help strengthen you against them? (See those listed in the endnotes for this section.)

K. Practice the Ordinances of God. Read ¶ 15 and the sidebar note "ordinances of God," pages 27–28. These ordinances are also referred to as the instituted means of grace, or Christian practices. Brainstorm for four or five minutes and list as many examples of specific Christian practices as you can. Then look for logical categories into which you can cluster the practices (such as compassion, justice, worship, devotion).

Choose one or two practices that are new (or atypical) for you. With a partner or two, covenant some specific way you can practice those ordinances during the next week or month. Agree on how you will check in and support each other in maintaining the practice for the designated time, and then how you will reflect on what difference, if any, it has made for you. (You will work with this in the next section, as well.)

L. Commission Your Covenant. Commission your covenant by saying with your partner(s) one of the three hymn fragments in ¶ 16, on pages 28–30.

Section III

The general theme of Section III is Wesley's teaching and review of sanctification (Christian perfection) with the pastors at three different conferences.

M. Engage in Christian Conferencing. Throughout your consideration of this section, imagine that you are John Wesley and his group of preachers (take turns being Wesley), and that you are together for mutual support, renewal, theological reflection, and accountability for your ministry. Above all, remember that you are together in love, not judgment. Whatever is said or done must be upbuilding in some way. Consider the questions in ¶ 17 (pages 33–37) that deal with sanctification. Also consider substantive questions that you identify regarding "how it is with your souls" and with your ministry, including the Christian practices you agreed upon in the previous section, for example:

- In what ways have you loved God with heart, mind, and soul?
- What has tempted you to fail to love in some way, and what have you done to resist that temptation?
- What Scriptures, spiritual friends, and Christian practices have helped you in your daily walk with God?
- How have you shared your faith with someone else since you last met? Whose testimony has inspired you and in what way?
- How have you kept your agreed-upon Christian practices and with what result? What support do you need?
- What gifts do you have, and what gifts have you employed, for the good of the church and community? (Feel free to identify the gifts you see in others.)

Inquire also about joys and concerns, and make time to pray about them. Plan to spend at least thirty to forty minutes in this examination and make use of the Scripture references in your reflection. If the group is large, form smaller groups of no more than six or seven persons.

N. Share Your Own Insights. After the initial examination, share any of your own ideas, convictions, or information that nurtured your relationship in the "connexion" and with God. If you would like to continue this experience, consider establishing a Covenant Discipleship Group. See *Guide for Covenant Discipleship Groups*, by Gayle Turner Watson (Discipleship Resources, 2000).

O. Create Your Benediction. Conclude your time together by choosing one or more of the hymn verses (¶ 18, pages 37–39) that speak to your own situation before God. Write the verse or verses on an index card or piece of paper to keep with you. Use the verse or verses as a prayer or benediction now and for the days ahead.

Section IV

The general theme of Section IV is how to recognize when someone has gone on to perfection in this life.

P. Tell About Your Faith Experience. Begin with a brief time for telling one another how you have lived and worked to have your mind fully in Christ since your last meeting. Use the list of five judgments of those "who met at Bristol" (page 42, mid-page) to evaluate what beliefs, thoughts, or actions were mistakes or evidence of sin. Discuss what Wesley means that "those who are most perfect have constant need of the merits of Christ." What difference do the merits of Christ make in your life, day by day?

Q. Understand and Illustrate John 15. Read John 15:1-11 and the two sets of five responses to the questions, Does a person living without sin continue to need a Mediator? Does he or she cease to need Christ in his priestly office? (pages 42–43). First discuss the offices of Jesus Christ in order to be clear about these general ways of understanding how he relates to humankind. (See the sidebars on pages 42 and 87.) How would you explain the priestly office or mediation of Jesus Christ on our behalf? What does it mean to you? On page 43, how does Wesley distinguish actual sins from faults or mistakes? How does his distinction here affect your own journey toward perfection in love?

Create a visual representation of the vine and branch image in John 15. This could be an artistic rendering of the text, an "organizational chart" with Jesus at the head, a flow chart showing cause and effect of abiding or not abiding in love, or something of your own choosing. Can you see yourself in this illustration? How does this illustrate (or not illustrate) your relationship with Jesus Christ? How might you rework the illustration to show your actual, and your hoped for, relationship with Christ and with others in the Christian community?

R. Examine Marks of Christian Perfection. The remainder of Section IV contains a series of questions about how one might know if another person has attained Christian perfection in his or her lifetime. These are some of the key points:

- Should one speak of this attainment? (pages 44–45)
- What is reasonable proof? (pages 45–46)
- What danger is there in pleasure? (page 46)
- What obstacles might prevent me from seeing the perfection of another? (pages 47–48)
- How does one judge what it means to be dead to sin? (pages 48–49)
- How should one treat those who think themselves perfected? (page 50–51)

Read in Suchocki's theological comment the entire section "Christian Perfection in Practice," pages 118–120, about how perfection operates (or doesn't) in our daily lives.

Form several small groups to examine each of these topics and consider these questions, using the following questions to guide your discussion. Look up the Scriptures in the endnotes that fall within the pages cited above, and discuss how they persuade you of Wesley's argument.

Speaking: What are the potential benefits and liabilities of speaking of such attainment? If a person has attained such holiness of heart, one might assume that his or her witness would be edifying, not self-aggrandizing. Can you think of anyone whose life witness is inspiring? How has that witness influenced you?

Seeking Proof: What might be the point of requiring or expecting proof that one is saved from all sin? What might be the danger in not asking for some kind of proof or explanation? What proof can you offer for your own spiritual life? Would the experience of fear or doubt contradict spiritual maturity? Why or why not?

Pleasure: What, do you think, is the place of pleasure in your spiritual development? Is something pleasurable necessarily tempting or inherently sinful or counter to God? Why? How can pleasure inspire or attract one to the Christian faith?

Obstacles: Think about the obstacles to Christian perfection and to recognizing such holiness in another person. What can be done to overcome these obstacles? Do you think this is possible in your own life? Why or why not?

Death to sin: What is inbred sin? What does it mean to be dead to sin? How would you describe the testimony of the Spirit? While God's perfecting action may be instantaneous, personal renewal is most often a process of growth in grace. How would you describe the gradual, day-by-day changes that might take place? In your own spiritual journey, what incremental steps do you see toward a more intimate relationship with God?

Treating the "Perfect": How would you regard someone who claims to have attained perfection in love? If you are this spiritually mature, what has been your experience of how others have regarded you? Spend some time reflecting on the harm or grief that our harsh judgments have inflicted on those who are on their own way to God. What does Wesley say to you about the course of dealing graciously with others?

S. Share and Compare Insights. Compare notes from the findings and insight from each discussion group, and choose one or two points that urge you onward in your own journey toward Christian perfection. Sing or say together "Jesus, Thine All-Victorious Love" (*The United Methodist Hymnal*, 422).

Section V

The general theme of Section V is the personal stories of those who have experience of Christian perfection.

T. Celebrate Pivotal Moments. Read ¶¶ 20 and 21 (pages 53–54). Has there been some pivotal year or moment in which you saw "a great increase in the work of God" either in your own life or in the community? Describe that experience. What did you think and feel? What prompted that moment? In the aftermath, what distortions or doubts occurred? Can you attribute them to Satan sowing "weeds among the wheat of Christ"? Why or why not?

Note Wesley's friend's comment on "limiting the Almighty" (¶ 21). What does it say to you about the way God works in the world? in your life? How would you describe the difference between God's "usual method" and God's "sovereign will"? What opportunities do you see in the faith community and in your life for "improvement in the spiritual life"?

U. Respond to Wesley's Questions. Read ¶¶ 22 and 23 (pages 54–55). In seven small teams, consider questions 1 through 22 in ¶ 23 as follows:

- Group 1—questions 1 and 2
- Group 2—questions 3 and 4

- Group 3—questions 5 through 7
- Group 4—questions 8 through 12
- Group 5—questions 13 through 16
- Group 6—questions 17 through 20
- Group 7—questions 21 and 22

With your understanding of Christian perfection so far, how would you respond to the questioner?

V. Seek Inspiration From Stories. Spend most of your time in this section with the personal stories. Imagine yourself a friend of Jane Cooper, who has sent the "memorial" in ¶ 24 (pages 56–57) to you. In small groups of two or three, talk about what Jane's story means to you, how it has affected or may affect your life, how it speaks to your soul and spirit, and how it recalls a story or other experience of your own with God. After each team member has spoken, spend two minutes in silence just to rest in God's presence.

Suchocki provides a theological commentary on personal perfection. See the sections "The Effects of Christian Perfection" and "Christian Perfection: Wesley's Lifelong Conviction," in Chapter 2, pages 120–123. However much this may help your understanding, though, use it only as a faint backdrop for the personal, affective approach to this activity.

W. Join the Eyewitnesses. Next look at the eyewitness account (the remainder of ¶ 24, pages 57–59). It appears in ¶¶ 1 through 4 that Jane was having what could be described as a mystical experience of God, a kind of union that transcends earthly explanation. Imagine yourself by her side, hearing this account. What did that experience seem to mean to her? What does it mean to you? Have you ever had this kind of union with God? If so, tell a partner about it (if you wish). Or take a few minutes to write a journal entry about it.

X. Keep Vigil. Paragraphs 5 through 10 (pages 58–59) report on Jane's last few days as friends kept vigil with her. Again, imagine that you are one of these trusted friends. What are you thinking and feeling as you witness Jane dying well? What legacy is she leaving her friends in attendance? Have you had an actual experience like this? If so, what treasure of faith was presented to you?

Read the Scriptures that sustained her (those mentioned and quoted in the text of her letter; see endnotes for references) and the surrounding verses for context. Jane suffered greatly, yet her faith carried her through. What Scriptures sustain you or hold you in love, especially when life is difficult?

Have you found Jesus to be a trusted friend to you in times of struggle or pain? How might you strengthen your relationship with Jesus Christ so that you experience his ongoing sustenance?

Y. Read and Sing of Love. Close by reading aloud 1 Corinthians 13:1-13 and singing "Love Divine, All Loves Excelling" (*The United Methodist Hymnal*, 384).

Section VI

The general theme of Section VI is the biblical and theological basis that establishes the core of what it means to be perfected, that is, renewed in God's love, with advice on how to keep from falling away from that love. It begins with ¶ 25.

Z. Study Law, Love, Need, Temptation. Paragraph 25 is a lengthy series of questions and answers that continues into Section VIII. Though there is overlap, questions 1–3 (pages 61–62) speak about the law; questions 4–8 (pages 62–63) discuss love; questions 9–13 (pages 63–65) deal with the need for Christ; and questions 14–21 (pages 65–68) concern temptation and corruption. Form four small groups to consider these issues and the Scripture references mentioned. Use the questions that follow as discussion starters.

You may want to check the endnotes for other references that Wesley did not identify in the text. How do they further the explanation of what it means to go on to perfection? What questions are raised for you in your own experience and understanding of this faith journey? After the smaller groups have met, come together to compare and discuss your responses.

- **Law:** What is the distinction between Mosaic law, adamic law, angelic law, and the law of faith? What does it mean to be "dead to the law"? Since the coming of Christ, how are we to understand the law and its influence on us? (For further consideration, see Suchocki's theological reflection on Question 1, beginning with the paragraph "Wesley had a grand scheme . . ." and the two paragraphs following it, page 106.)

- **Love:** How does love fulfill the law? How would you describe the fruits or properties of this love? How are mistakes understood (as opposed to sin)? (See also Suchocki's theological commentary beginning at the bottom of page 112 with the paragraph, "And so Wesley says that we now . . ." and going through the end of Chapter 1 on page 114.)

- **Need for Christ:** In what ways do we need Christ? What role does the Atonement play in our process of Christian perfection? What is the difference between sincerity and Christian perfection?

- **Temptation and Corruption:** What is the distinction between temptation and corruption of the heart? How does sanctification overcome temptation and corruption? How does Scripture help us understand how Christian perfection is possible in a world of sin and corruption?

AA. Illustrate a Lack of the Fruit of the Spirit. First look at Wesley's diagnosis of those who are somehow lacking in the fruit of the Spirit and who "grieve the Holy Spirit." Read Galatians 5:6-21 and questions 27 and 28 (pages 69–71). In five small groups, review how Wesley describes those who are lacking in gentleness, goodness, fidelity, meekness, and temperance. In each small group, draw a composite picture of a person, church, community, or nation lacking in one of these gifts of the Spirit. Be both general and specific in your portrait.

BB. Create a Social Map. Next go back to read questions 22–26 (pages 68–69) and Galatians 5:22-26. One who lives completely in the fruit of the Spirit is both justified and sanctified, and generally this happens as a process. Together create a "social map" from today onward. Imagine that everyone in your portrait is surely going on to perfection. Describe, draw, create a song, or write in a journal about what things look like today, in two years, in five years, in ten years, and so on. Be both general and specific. How might the world (or neighborhood) look near the end of your lives? What social conventions and institutions, including the church, will change and how? Invite the groups to compare their portraits and their conclusions.

CC. Growing In and Falling From Grace. Read questions 29–31, on pages 71–72. By God's grace we may attain Christian perfection, but then we must never relax our vigilance lest we fall. Perfection is not a goal to attain nor a prize to keep, but a minute-by-minute way of life. How, in your Christian journey, do you see steps of maturation in faith? How do you keep from being discouraged if you miss the mark? Does desiring and ordering your life toward Christian perfection seem like a chore that never ends or a blessing to enjoy when it comes, or something else? What, in your estimation, is God's grace worth to you?

DD. Sing About Principles. Close your time together by singing or saying "I Want a Principle Within" (*The United Methodist Hymnal*, 410).

Section VII

The general theme of Section VII is advice given to those who have fallen from grace. Chapter 3 of Suchocki's theological reflection, "Advices" (pages 125–134), expands the theological commentary on this advice.

EE. Sing About Jesus. Begin this section by singing or saying together "Jesus! The Name High Over All" (*The United Methodist Hymnal*, 193).

FF. Keep From Falling From Grace. Form five new groups to consider the first five pieces of advice Wesley offers those who would protect themselves from falling from grace. Review together as necessary questions 29–31 (pages 71–72), then in the five groups review questions 32–36 (pages 73–78), one question per group. Use the following questions as discussion/reflection starters. Look up the Scriptures (and surrounding verses for context) that are cited in each question, per the endnotes. Take several minutes all together to compare your insights on the nature and consequence of each of these sins.

- **Pride:** If you know you have attained to the mind of Christ and want to share that with others, how is that distinguished from pridefulness? How would you describe the relationship between grace and light? (See also the sidebar on page 53 and Suchocki's comments on "The First Advice: Beware of Pride," pages 125–127.)

- **Enthusiasm:** What is enthusiasm? What is the difference between pride and enthusiasm? How can you recognize the "device of Satan" that expects the ends without the means? (See also the sidebar on page 53 and Suchocki's comments on "The Second Advice: Beware of Enthusiasm," pages 127–129.)

- **Antinomianism:** What is antinomianism? What is the role of bigotry, self-indulgence, intolerance, and solifidianism in moral law and the law of love? (See also the sidebar note on page 77 and Suchocki's comments on "The Third Advice: Beware of Antinomianism," pages 129–131.)

- **Sins of Omission:** How can we be judged for what we do not do? How many opportunities do you leave unimproved each day? How might a review of your day or week reveal missed opportunities for doing good? (See also Suchocki's comments on "The Fourth Advice: Beware of Sins of Omission," page 131.)

• **Desiring Only God:** Take an inventory of a typical day to review how often your thoughts are on something other than God. How can we orient our lives at work, home, school, and play to "desire only God"? What would that look like to you? (See Suchocki's comments on "The Fifth Advice: Beware of Desiring Anything But God," pages 131–132.)

Next, working privately and in silence, take five minutes or so to think, write, and pray about how you may be engaging in the sin mentioned in your group's question (or one of the others, if you wish) and how God can work in your life to lead you from falling away from grace.

GG. Write Ten Commandments of Unity. Read question 37 (the sixth advice, on pages 78–80; see also Suchocki's comments on "The Sixth Advice: Beware of Schism," pages 132–133), which offers important advice about avoiding schism or separation in the church or in society. (Wesley would argue that unity is not debatable for the church, since the church's central role is as the unified, holistic body of Christ, regardless of how imperfectly that role may be lived out.) First identify and write on a chalkboard or newsprint Wesley's main points so that they can be seen easily by all. Look up the Scriptures (and surrounding verses for context) that are noted. Using these words of advice from Wesley and from the Bible, make up your own Ten Commandments of church unity. Invite each person to rank the commandments according to how crucial that advice is, first for your congregation and then for The United Methodist Church, with 10 being most crucial and 1 being least crucial. Tally the rankings.

In three small groups, discuss the top three rankings for the local church and for The United Methodist Church, one local commandment and one United Methodist commandment per group. Note that Wesley urges confession for those who fall short. Discuss why your group's commandment is so important, what is done or not done that contributes to its importance, and what failings need to be confessed. Name three practical, achievable things you can do as a church or as individuals to follow that commandment faithfully. Compare your findings, write them down, and collect them.

HH. Be Exemplary. Read this first part of question 38, on page 80. Make a beginning, cursory list of (1) the outward things; (2) the little things; (3) the regard and use of money; (4) the things you take in

earnest; and (5) the usefulness of your life in the world, with an eye to finding exemplary ways to fulfill them. What attitudes and behaviors do you brush over or ignore that might be brought into an exemplary life for God? (See also Suchocki's brief theological comment on "The Seventh Advice: Be Exemplary in All Things," pages 133–134.)

II. Offer Commitments to God. Close this section by commending to God the discoveries and commitments regarding your local congregation, The United Methodist Church, and your personal lives. Read aloud 2 Peter 1:3-11 as a benediction and reminder of God's desires and promise for us.

Section VIII

The general theme of Section VIII completes ¶ 25 with a review of eight theological reflections on the life that is ordered according to the mind of Christ, after which Wesley determines that he has done what he proposed. In this session (or in a separate Session IX) you will propose how to follow through on your own journey toward Christian perfection.

JJ. Sing About Peace in Christ. Begin this section by singing or saying together "Thou Hidden Source of Calm Repose" (*The United Methodist Hymnal*, 153).

KK. Reflections on Wesley's Last Advice. Wesley's "last advice" (question 38, at the end of Section VII, page 80) is supported in eight reflections (pages 81–86) that deal with general advice, the place of suffering, humility, love of others, prayer, following the "narrow way," vigilance, and the life of service. Individually select the reflection that seems the most difficult or foreign for you. (Those who select the same point can work together.) Use these questions as necessary to begin your own reflection. If you wish, do this as a journaling exercise. After working with the reflection that seems most difficult, choose one or two others and continue your assessment of your own progress of sanctification.

1. "The most direct way God uses to draw us to God is to afflict us in the thing we love most, and with good reason." What does this mean? How might it be true for you?

2. Are you "thoroughly willing that God should treat you in the manner that is pleasing to God . . . without complaining"? How can you tell if what you suffer is what God wills or is a result of sin—yours or another's?

3. "There is no love of God without patience, and no patience without humility and sweetness of spirit." Is this true? Is this true for you? Do you have the patience for true humility and the sweetness of spirit for true patience?

4. "Tolerating others and suffering evils in meekness and silence is the sum of a Christian life." Is this so? Is this something you can do and are willing to do? Why or why not?

5. Prayer, and the life of constant prayer, are defined in several ways. Have you recognized prayer in these ways? Is your prayer life more expansive than you thought? If your prayer life is modest, in what ways do you invite God to act in your life and then see that happening?

6. God cares about the smallest of things. What might be some of the "troubles that sometimes flow from those faults that appear to be minor failings"? How might excesses of body contribute to the insensitivity of your soul?

7. "The devil never enters more dangerously than by small, unnoticed events that seem to be insignificant. Yet they gradually open the heart to great temptations." (I guess the devil is in the details!) Do you think this is true? What "insignificant" port of entry is wide open for sin in your life?

8. "One of the cardinal rules of religion is to lose no opportunity to serve God . . . in our neighbor." What opportunities have you left unimproved? What opportunities do you seize?

LL. Let the "Sparks" Fly. "Sparks From the Fire," Chapter 4 of Suchocki's theological reflection, deals with the eight reflections from activity "KK" in a different way. Read the introduction to this chapter together (page 135), then consider the "sparks," either together or by dividing them among small groups.
- Prayer as participation in God's creative power (pages 135–138)
- Bearing the faults of others and our own faults (pages 138–139)
- Praying without ceasing (pages 139–141)
- Corporate prayer connecting the body of Christ (pages 141–142)
- Offering our good works as prayer (pages 142–144)

Read each segment of the chapter and the related text from Wesley's *A Plain Account*. Examine the theological commentary for each spark and use these questions as discussion/reflection starters:
- What is Dr. Suchocki saying?
- Do you agree or disagree with her? Why?

- What "aha" moments have her comments elicited (and if not "aha," then perhaps "uh oh")?
- What practical implications do these reflections offer in your own spiritual life and behavior?

Use the index in *The United Methodist Hymnal* to identify the hymns of Charles and John Wesley. Review the hymns to see how these comments are reflected in the Wesleys' hymnody. Sing or say together one or more of the hymns.

MM. Review Christian Perfection. Read Paragraph 26 on pages 86–87. Spend a few minutes reviewing and clarifying Wesley's thoughts on Christian perfection. Recall the important insight gained from the previous sections and list some of them.

Read the four Scriptures underlined in question 26 and rewrite them in your own works. Add one or two promises of your own for how to behave your way into that way of being. Keep those promises where you will see and think about them.

These final activities can be included as options for Section VIII, though you are encouraged to plan for an extra session for these closing activities. The Covenant Renewal Service will take about thirty minutes and should be preceded by some time of centering and reflection.

NN. Tell Your Own Stories. Spend most (but not all) of your time together telling your own stories. Who have you known who has most embodied the character of a perfected Christian? Which insight and Scriptures have been the most powerful, even transforming, for you? What, if anything, has encouraged you to a greater dedication to living a life centered in Jesus Christ? In what new ways do you hear God calling to you (individually or as a church) to be in devoted service?

OO. Develop Action Plans. After you have talked about your stories and sense of call, take time to develop some action plans, both personal and corporate. What specific, attainable, and measurable goals can you set that will move you and your church toward greater godliness in service and worship?

PP. Have a Covenant Renewal. Close by committing yourself to these goals using the Covenant Renewal Service (*The United Methodist Book of Worship*, 288). Include in the service "Jesus, United by Thy Grace" (*The United Methodist Hymnal*, 561). Continue in your covenant by forming Covenant Discipleship Groups (see "N," on page 95).

A Plain Account of
A Plain Account of Christian Perfection
Theologically Considered

by Marjorie Hewitt Suchocki

Contents

A Plain Account of *A Plain Account of Christian Perfection* Theologically Considered
by Marjorie Hewitt Suchocki

Introduction
My Journey
From There to Here

I was not always a United Methodist. In fact, my ecclesial journey took me through many denominations over the years. My family was not a "church-going" family, so I was sent rather than brought to Sunday school. In my little New England town, that Sunday school was Congregational. My best friend in high school was a Nazarene girl, so I went with her on Sunday evenings to her holiness church—with no idea at all that her denomination traced its heritage back to this little book that I later came to regard as the most astonishing theological book I had ever read. When I decided to go to college at age 20, it was to a Wesleyan Methodist college in upstate New York. Once again I was immersed in a culture deeply affected by Wesley's little book.

I married, and that began years of frequent moves. With every move, our little family simply looked for the closest church that felt like "home," and joined it. Consequently, I was for six months a Nazarene, for two years an old-style Presbyterian (long since merged into its successor denominations), for one year a Baptist, and then for ten years a member of a nondenominational community church. Another move brought me into the Missouri Synod Lutheran Church, and by then I had started graduate studies. My studies clashed with a church where I heard, from a respected college dean, that if I didn't believe that God created the world in six days then I did not believe in Jesus Christ. And so with the next move, I became a member of the American Lutheran Church. The following move found me living across the street from an Episcopalian church where, wonder of wonders, one of the ministers was a woman! And so I promptly became an Episcopalian.

By that time, I was teaching theology in a Presbyterian school and also directing a Doctor of Ministry program. This latter work brought me to the attention of the administration of Wesley Theological Seminary in Washington, DC, who asked me to be their academic dean. Prayer and deliberation led me to accept the offer.

But then I was faced with the conundrum that led me to become a United Methodist. In 1983, there had never been a woman dean of a United Methodist seminary. Neither had Wesley seminary ever had a layperson as dean, or, for that matter, someone who was not United Methodist. Meanwhile, I had observed some of the miscommunications that occurred when the dean of a school did not share the denomination of the school—and after all, I had moved around a bit. So I decided that the first two of these three "it's never been done that way before" were non-negotiable—I am a laywoman. But if they would have me, I certainly could be a United Methodist. After all, why not? I'd already been connected with all those other denominations; I was a walking ecumenist! To my surprise, I found that the president of the school was absolutely delighted with the idea of my becoming United Methodist, even for these quite pragmatic reasons. And so in January of 1984, being newly arrived in Washington, DC, I joined Metropolitan Memorial United Methodist Church. At last, I was a Methodist!

As a United Methodist dean, I discovered a wonderful custom called pastors' school. Bishops, taking their teaching authority seriously, called all the pastors from a conference together for the specific purpose of theological or biblical or historical study. *Splendid*, I thought. And then in the spring of 1984, the call came to me from the West Virginia Annual Conference: "Please come teach a pastors' school for us." "Of course," answered I. "We'd like you to teach John Wesley's little book, *A Plain Account of Christian Perfection*." *Why not?* thought I, even though I had never read John Wesley, much less this little book. But it was a little book; surely I could do it. I agreed.

And that is when my heart was, as they say, strangely warmed. As I read the book, I was clearly astonished. Could he actually be saying that? Did he mean it? He did! John Wesley actually thought that God created us to be in God's image, and this image involved using all our powers to God's glory, which is sheer love. This in itself may not seem so astonishing, but what Wesley did next is what stunned me. He taught that since that is what God wants, that is what God makes possible for us in Jesus Christ. That is, the purpose of salvation is to get on with the adventure of fulfilling God's purposes; and by God, there is grace enough to accomplish it. We can live fully, to the glory of God, in this life, not just the next. Clearly, Wesley was not a "pie in the sky by and by" man. *Why*, thought I, *this is the merriest theologian I have ever read,* and I became a "heart" Methodist on the spot. And I say with confidence that while it may have taken a circuitous route to get me here, I will never be anything other than United Methodist, by God's grace.

Since that time nearly twenty years ago I have read much in Wesley's writings; and in fact, I taught Methodist Doctrine at Claremont School of Theology following the retirement of my colleague, Professor Jack Verheyden. Methodist Doctrine was my favorite course. But no matter how much I read of Wesley, I never found him to depart from the wonder of his teaching in that one small book, *A Plain Account of Christian Perfection.* Christian perfection seemed to me to be the heart of his teaching and, consequently, absolutely central to what it means to be a United Methodist.

When I attended my first ordination service at an annual conference, I listened joyously to the question asked of each ordinand, "Do you intend to press on to perfection in this life?" But an oddity occurred. I discovered through the years that few United Methodists had actually read this astonishing little book. "How can this be?" queried I. The answers are various, but I think they come down to these things. First of all, this eighteenth-century book is not written in ways that are comfortable to twenty-first-century Christians. There are words in the text that no longer mean what they did in Wesley's time, which can make the text hard to understand. Second, the very word *perfection* is still a stumbling block, as it was in Wesley's day. Again and again and again he explains that what he means by perfection is simply the love of God and neighbor

filling the heart and life. But despite his laborious explanations, what the word actually communicated to its hearers was a sort of "holier than thou" stance indicating that one never made any mistakes at all. I fervently wished Wesley had stuck with the word *love* instead of *perfection*, since that's what he meant. But, of course, Wesley thought that love was perfect, so *perfection* was a perfectly adequate word. Finally, it is quite probable that my long background in reading and teaching theology made a difference to my reading the text. Without such a background, it might be hard to see the underlying structure of the text and to pick out the central points.

In 2003 the first of these problems was addressed. Steven W. Manskar led the United Methodist General Board of Discipleship in developing a contemporary version of Wesley's *A Plain Account of Christian Perfection*. This modern-language version clarifies outdated words, supplies the context that explains Wesley's references, and suggests how different statements might relate to Wesley's larger theological vision. In short, *A Plain Account of Christian Perfection* now exists in a far more readable edition in this book called *A Perfect Love: Understanding John Wesley's "A Plain Account of Christian Perfection."*

And so with great and merry daring, I am writing a theological companion to the book. My hope is that people within the Wesleyan tradition—and certainly United Methodists—will pick up this book and join me and the General Board of Discipleship in celebrating the theological heart of our tradition. But, of course, celebrating this heart of our tradition is not simply a head trip. It is answering, as do those ordinands, "Yes, I am, by God's grace, pressing on to Christian perfection!"

Chapter One
The Heart of the Matter

Begin with Section VI. "Why not begin at the beginning?" you might very reasonably ask. To which I answer, "We are!" It is just that the nub of Wesley's understanding of Christian perfection, from which all else follows, is right here almost at the center of the book. And so my structure for this theological companion to *A Plain Account of Christian Perfection* begins with Wesley's reasons outlining why he advocates Christian perfection. There is an amazing theology contained in these few pages.

Following this, in Chapter Two, we will go back and look at Wesley's descriptions, explanations, exasperations, and clarifications that are contained primarily in the first half of the book, culminating in his extensive example of Jane Cooper, a woman whom he believed manifested Christian perfection in her life (Sections I–V).

In Chapter Three we will move on to Wesley's seven "advices" to those who would seek Christian perfection (pages 73–80).

Finally, in Chapter Four, we will conclude, as did Wesley, with the implications of Christian perfection for the life of prayer. It is not that Wesley suddenly switched gears and began a sustained theological treatise on a theology of prayer. Rather, it is more as if his sustained thinking on Christian perfection led him naturally to make a number of rather astonishing references to prayer as he concluded the book—almost like his own "amen" to the prayer that all who are called Methodists shall be open to the gift of God's love. In this final chapter we will gather up his nuggets on prayer, weaving them into both a conclusion and a beginning—a conclusion to this particular book, but an everlasting beginning to probing the possibilities of prayer and perfection.

Created for the Glory of God

So, then, turn to page 61, paragraph number 25, which begins a series of questions numbered 1 through 38 (pages 61–80). Our attention focuses here on questions 1 through 6, but the critical paragraph is the answer to question 1, as follows:

> In order to understand this [how Christ is the end of the law for righteousness to every one that believes], you must understand what law is spoken of here. This I understand is (1) the Mosaic law, the whole Mosaic system, which Saint Paul repeatedly speaks of as one, though containing three parts: the political, moral, and ceremonial. (2) The Adamic law was given to Adam in innocence and is properly called "the law of works." This is in substance the same as the angelic law, being common to angels and humans. It required that humans should use, to the glory of God, all the powers with which they were created. Now, they were

created free from any defect, either in understanding or affections. The human body was then no impediment to the mind. It did not hinder clearly understanding all things, judging truly concerning them, and reasoning justly, if they reasoned at all. I say "if they reasoned," for possibly they did not. Perhaps they had no need of reasoning until their corruptible bodies pressed down the mind and impaired their natural abilities. Perhaps until then, the mind saw every truth as directly as the eye now sees the light.

Consequently, this law, proportioned to their original powers, required that they should always think, always speak, and always act precisely right, in every possible point. They were very able to do so. God could not but require the service they were able to give.

But Adam fell.

Wesley has a grand scheme of creation in mind. Imagine it! The God of all the universe spins a world into space for the single purpose of creating such creatures as the Adam whom Wesley describes in this text. It matters not if we, instead of visualizing a single-minded creation, now think of a magnificently profligate God spinning all kinds of bodies into space at the dawn of this current universe. Perhaps, indeed, there are many purposes in the divine mind for such a multifaceted, intensely complex, ultimately relational universe as ours. Regardless, what Wesley tells us in this passage is his notion of what God intended in calling humans into existence, and this is significant indeed.

God created us in order that we should use all the powers with which we were created to the glory of God. And what are these powers? Wesley spells them out: they are intellectual, attitudinal, and physical.

We know this quite well; we are reasoning creatures, feeling creatures, embodied creatures. Wesley suggests that the fullest development of these powers leads to the glory of God. Before we talk about just what this "glory of God" is, think into the radical implications of this text. The import of the text is not just to satisfy our intellectual curiosity about what a supposed first human would be like; rather, it calls us to a vision of what we should be like. Again and again Wesley tells us that the work of Christ is to restore the image of God in us, to give us a "new Eden" (see the lines of the Charles Wesley hymn on page 15: "My heart, thou know'st, can never rest / Till thou create my peace, / Till, of my Eden repossessed, / From every sin I cease"). Wesley's description of God's intentions in Adam are directly appropriate to his understanding of God's intentions for us in Christ.

Wesley seems to me to be quite radical here, almost foreseeing what would become liberation theology in the twentieth century. Unfortunately, there is a long tradition within Christian history of devaluing the fullest development of our minds, hearts, and bodies—especially bodies. Flagellation of bodies in order to keep bodily instincts under control is but one of the most egregious examples of this. And there are far too many writings within the Christian tradition where it seems that there is a direct correlation between a low regard for humanity and a high regard for God. It is as if the very honor of God requires the abasement of the creature; God is great to the degree that creatures are lowly. Is this the glory of God? Not for Wesley.

Wesley's view is quite contrary to this reasoning. God creates the human for the sake of flourishing, of full development, and this development tends toward God's glory. A rather homely analogy could be drawn from our own experience. Whom do we honor more, the cook whose soufflés always fall or the cook whose perfectly done soufflés win prizes every time? "What a cook!" we say. Or consider the example of art. I have tried my hand at oils a time or two, and believe me, my results will never make it to the Los Angeles County Museum of Art without my smuggling them in. Nobody would look at my painting and say, "What a terrific artist she is!" But consider a Monet painting, or a Rembrandt. We are awestruck, marveling at the creative power of the artist. We honor artists like them precisely because of the beauty of their work, and we call them masters.

Our Intellectual Powers

God the creator is not glorified through our denigration but through the wonder of who we were created to be. God created us with minds, and calls us to develop them to the fullest. We are to rejoice in our "mindedness" and learn all we can, pushing our abilities to the very limit. The fun, of course, is that once we find a limit, our limit expands and there is yet more to learn.

I remember when I was a young woman, newly returning to college in my thirties after my youngest child was enrolled in school. I took a philosophy class and was enthralled with what I was learning. I could hardly wait to read the books, listen to lectures, and think about these wonders I was newly finding. My whole being, it seemed, was awakened through this wonder of the life of the mind. As a religious young woman, I began to worry: was it possible, was it barely possible, that my love for studying could rival my love for God? Was I setting up an "idol," and should I cease studying immediately in order to keep my love in its proper channels? I prayed over this issue and finally told God that if God did not want me to study, God would have to stop me, because I simply was not capable of stopping myself.

Reading Wesley made me recall that early agony with joyous laughter. Of course God did not consider my development of my mind as somehow standing in competition with my love of God. To the contrary, God called me to such study. I was endowed with reason for the purpose of developing reason. And to the extent that I cooperated with God in developing my reason, I honored God the creator.

Our Attitudinal Powers

Perhaps it is not unusual for a theologian to push us to develop our abilities to reason. But Wesley names affections and bodies as also being part of the powers with which we were created. If we understand affections as our whole attitudinal life, including our emotions, then the implication is that our emotions, too, are not given to us in order to be stunted. To the contrary, we are to rejoice in our emotional life, developing our affections in openness to the love of God. The richer our emotional capacities, the greater are our capacities to give and receive love toward and from God and others.

Our Physical Powers

And are not our bodies, too, a wondrous thing? The apostle Paul even calls our bodies temples of the Spirit of God. Having been endowed with bodies, we are to develop our bodies to the fullest of their powers, to the glory of God. The implications of this are certainly practical. It means we are bound to take care of our physical selves with healthy diets, exercise, and proper rest. We are to honor the sexuality that God has given us, developing this as well as our other aspects to the glory of God. As the psalmist said, we are "fearfully and wonderfully made" (139:14). Thus our attitude toward our embodiedness should be gratitude, joy, and the discipline to develop our bodies to the fullest extent possible given our circumstances.

Developing Our God-Given Powers

In short, a Wesleyan understanding of what it is to be human considers our intelligence, emotions, and bodies all to be a gift from God, and thus we honor God insofar as we gratefully develop the gift as much as possible within our circumstances. And this, of course, leads to two more considerations: First, we must ask a bit further about what this "glory of God" means, since it is the end term of how we should develop the powers with which we were created. Second, we must pay more attention to that word Wesley introduces, *impediments*, which arise because of that final sentence I quoted, "But Adam fell."

To the Glory of God

I have already said that to develop all of our powers is to honor the God who endowed us with these powers, and I have implied that to honor God is to glorify God. But what does it mean, this glorification? For Wesley there is a depth of meaning to the "glory of God" that goes far beyond paying compliments to God, or even showing through our beings what a wonderful Creator God is. The glory of God is, finally, nothing other than the love of God. God's deepest being is constituted by an enormous profundity of love, beyond anything that the human heart can fully comprehend. To gaze directly into the shining love of God would be equivalent to gazing directly at the sun; like Moses of old, our faces must be veiled. And yet this boundless love is the very depths of God, the character of God, and therefore also the glory of God. Thus when Wesley says that we are to develop all our powers to the glory of God, he is saying that God's love is the criterion we use for the development of our powers.

There is a wonderful Wesleyan hymn built around the image of Jacob wrestling with the angel by night; only we are the ones who wrestle with this strange adversary. "Come, O Thou Traveler Unknown" (*United Methodist Hymnal*, 386 and 387) portrays us alone in the night, wrestling with one whose name we do not know. Throughout the hymn we demand the name of this wrestler. "I need not tell thee who I am," we cry, for the wrestler knows us all too well; our names are written on the palms of his hands. But who is he? The hymn skirts the issue, daring it and backing away: "I will not let thee go till I thy name, thy nature know." But gradually the knowledge becomes more sure, till finally at the last we cry again and again, "Thy nature and thy name is Love."

God is a pure fountain of love—not abstractly, not philosophically, not in isolated splendor. Rather, God's very nature is to love, and through loving, to elicit our own loving in return. Love is, of all things, relational; and the God whose name and nature is love is relational, through and through. Out of the depths of divine relation, God loves; and we are most wondrously created because of that love, and for that love, and toward that love.

Therefore, when it is stated that we are to develop all the powers with which we were created toward the glory of God, it is clear that there is an end besides self-development that is in view. Or, rather, self-development is for the sake of that which is beyond the self. And what is beyond the self? Everything is both infinitely and intimately beyond the self. How can this be? Think about it like this. Out of boundless love, God creates a world, and within that world there is at least one singular species that is capable of intentionally reflecting that love of God. This reflection of the love of God will not beam back to God like a laser, singly focused on loving just that one ultimate reality. Rather, just as God's love suffuses all creation, our love inspired by God's love is multidimensional. It is toward God in and through the creation that God loves; it is toward God out of the sheer answering love that God inspires in us; it is toward God simply because God is God, whose nature and whose name is Love. To develop all the powers with which we are created to the glory of God, then, is to develop ourselves fully for the sake not just of ourselves, but for God and all creation. There is a deep responsiveness and responsibility built into the call to develop ourselves to the glory of God, for it demands from us a joyous relationality, a profound yearning toward community, where there is giving and receiving of love.

Oddly enough, then—or perhaps not so oddly—we are bound together through developing our powers, for we enrich each other through our own richness of being. When the glory of God is the end of our development—or the beginning of our development—then self-development is at the same time communal development. And this is a joyous thing.

"But Adam Fell"

But then we come to the sadness of those three words, "But Adam fell." Wesley's view was that once Adam fell, God's glorious intent for creation was momentarily thwarted. I say "momentarily," for Wesley then moves quickly from the Adamic (and angelic) law of works to the Mosaic law of works. This is a compensating move. Adam was to develop himself voluntarily, but given his fall—and the fall of us all with him—voluntary development of all our powers in the context of the glory of God became exceedingly problematic. And so the Mosaic law becomes a kind of social channeling of the requirement that we should develop all our powers relationally, lovingly. Instead of depending upon voluntary obedience to this empowering command, we are given aids for obedience. These aids, says Wesley, are political, ceremonial, and moral.

In a sense, if we stretch our imaginations a bit, the political, ceremonial, and moral are like extensions into society of the physical, rational, and emotional. That is, we are embodied into political societies, are we not? And our ceremonial life is in a sense our rational life, our way of formulating the rituals of worship that explain our relationship to God. The moral, of course, is the way we relate to each other, like our attitudinal or emotional life. So in a loose sense, the individual law of works given to Adam now becomes a social structure, a communal law of works. And just as our own identity comes about through the development of our personal powers, our social identity comes about through how we conform to the structures designed to weld us together into community. If God is glorified as personal existence develops through love, then the social complement to this is that God is glorified insofar as social existence develops through justice. For justice is the effective channeling of love.

Thus in the Mosaic law of works we have one refrain that moves throughout the Pentateuch, bidding the society to care for the widow, the orphan, and the stranger within its gates. The justice of the society is measured by how effectively the society addresses the needs of those who are outside the normal channels of well-being in the patriarchal world. Insofar, then, as the society as a whole tends toward health, toward wisdom, toward morality, God's original intentions in creation are fulfilled. The society will be to the glory of God.

The hitch is that the society is no more successful than Adam in cooperating with the divine intentions. The paradox is that God's intentions are toward the finest well-being of the creature, but the creature acts against its own well-being. The law of works, whether through Adam or Moses, individual or society, does not succeed.

God's Intent Toward Us

At this point a contemporary reader of *A Plain Account* might raise a strong objection. "But there never was an Adam!" one might cry. In the eighteenth century, the radical discoveries of creation through evolution were hardly on the horizon; Adam was the best explanation for the human race—and human problems. There were certainly rumblings. On the philosophical scene, many an alternative was raised to account for the pervasive tendency of human beings to violate their own and others' well-being. But for Wesley and for many in the field of religion, the old story of Adam still had cogent power.

Does Wesley's understanding depend upon a historical Adam? My answer is, not at all. Adam becomes the package through which Wesley discerns the divine intent for creaturely well-being, an intent that is mediated through numerous texts other than those two small chapters in Genesis. The packing may fall away, but the content remains. Our best contemporary knowledge of the world suggests that Adam is a symbol projected back upon the mysteries and limits of the human sense of time. What Wesley reads into the Adamic story does not depend upon a historical Adam; it depends upon the gracious creative intent of God. Wesley's purpose is to say that this wondrous thing, this full development of all our powers in the context and toward the increase of the glory of God, is God's intent toward us, for us. And if it couldn't happen through a first human being, and if it couldn't happen through a model society, we are not left to despair; for it is in and through God's work in Jesus Christ that this wonderful reality is now made possible for us.

A New Possibility

The remarkable thing about Wesley is that he figured God could not be stopped by human recalcitrance. And human recalcitrance there is and was. Wesley understood that with Adam's fall, the development of all the powers with which Adam was created is seriously hindered, not only for Adam but for Adam's race. We no longer think clearly, and since our thinking is so often muddled, so are our judgments. "It is as natural," says Wesley, "for a human being to mistake as to breathe" (page 61). Likewise with our physical and emotional selves: we are not only frail and subject to illness and injury, but we hardly know how to love properly. We can fulfill neither the Adamic nor the Mosaic version of the command to develop all our powers fully to the glory of God.

But it is God who intends our good, and what God intends, by God, can and will happen! Jesus Christ becomes our Eden, our re-creation, our new possibility of finally becoming what God intended us to be: loving human beings in interlocking communities that foster the development of each for the good of all, to the glory of God. How does this happen? We turn once again to our text (pages 61–62). Given Adam's fall,

> . . . no human is able to perform the service that the Adamic law requires.
> No human is, of course, obliged to perform it. God does not require it of any human. For Christ is the end of the Adamic, as well as the Mosaic, law. By his death he has put an end to both. He has abolished both the one and the other, with regard to humankind. . . .
> In place of this, Christ has established another, namely, the law of faith. Not everyone who does, but everyone who believes, now receives righteousness in the full sense of the word. That is, they are justified, sanctified, and glorified.

Since we are no longer capable of following God's intents for us unaided, God's own self both clears our rubble-strewn pathway and enables us to walk upon it.

The Personal and Social Nature of Sin

Consider the nature of sin in a Wesleyan world. If God intended us to develop ourselves fully under the criterion of the love of God, then sin is anything that works against that goal. We can consider sin under the blanket category of disobedience, but disobedience alone is an empty category. It begs the question, Disobedience of what, and why? Here, it is an express disobedience to develop all one's powers to the glory of God, or under the criterion of love. This disobedience, then, is anything that flaunts either the fullest development of oneself or of others. Ultimately, of course, this disobedience directly violates the love of God.

Furthermore, we must take the Mosaic as well as the Adamic law of works into consideration. Too easily we turn sin into some personal issue only, as if we, like Wesley's Adam, are responsible only for our own development of our own powers. Not even Eve appears in these pages discussing Adam's sin. But Wesley quickly takes us into the social dimension of the law of works. Those political, ceremonial, and moral laws were for the sake of communal individuals. That is, on one hand the laws reinforced our weak abilities, helping us through social sanctions to develop all our powers toward the glory of God. But on the other hand, the social structure emphasizes the communal nature of self-development, so that the development of one is for the sake of the good of all, and the good of all is to be mediated to each. Everyone is responsible not only to the self but to others individually and to the society as a whole. We are communal individuals, or individuals-in-community, and the development of the self is contextualized by the development of others.

The disobedience of sin, then, must take account not only of the Adamic law of works, which easily tends to vaunt the individual alone. It must also take account of the Mosaic law, or the communal nature through which the development of all the powers with which we were created is to take place, to the glory of God. Commonly, we call the violations of the Mosaic law injustice. Sin, then, is both personal and social; and in both cases it is a violation of the love of God. And in both cases, sin refuses the intent of God toward our individual and communal good.

The Law of Faith

We can take this analysis one more step and note that God's intent toward us is toward the flourishing of life. We are, each one of us together, to develop our physical, mental, and emotional lives to the good of all. This would make for a thriving good, a communal life sparkling with health and good will. To live otherwise, then, is to live against the flourishing of life. It is, in sad fact, to live toward the destruction of such development; it is to live toward death.

The problem standing in the way of the fulfillment of God's command—both the Adamic and the Mosaic—is not only our disobedience, but the wreckage that accumulates along the way of our disobedience, a wreckage that makes toward death, not life. The connection of sin and death, then, is not arbitrary, but descriptive: to move against that which makes for the flourishing of life is by definition to act toward that which makes for the destruction of life. And this is the problem with which God must deal if God is to help us get on with our own good.

Again, the text (still on page 62):

> ...Christ has established another, namely, the law of faith. Not everyone
> who does, but everyone who believes, now receives righteousness in the full

sense of the word. That is, they are justified, sanctified, and glorified.

In one sense, it is not too much to say that for Wesley, the purpose of God's presence in Jesus Christ is to clear away the rubble that sin creates, making a path straight toward the accomplishment of the purposes of God. Sin, and the destruction and deaths that it entails, must be dealt with; otherwise, it remains the obstruction to God's purposes in creation. So in Wesley's view, God in Christ recreates the Adamic setting, only this time the new Adam fully lives up to God's intent. Jesus lives vibrantly, fully developing all the powers with which he was created toward the end of love, which glorifies God. And for Wesley, the life of Jesus as recorded in the gospels is as compellingly important as his birth, death, and resurrection. In and through Jesus, it is possible to see how an individual lives from and toward the love of God. Jesus has clarity about the purpose of all laws not to be ends in themselves but to be means to the end of the flourishing of life. Jesus exercises compassion. He gives of himself toward the empowerment of others. He forgives the sins that get in the way of being what we are called to be before God in community. For Wesley, Jesus simply "gets it right." He is the fulfillment of God's intent that we should develop all the powers with which we were created to the glory of God, and therefore he is also the clear example of what such a life would look like.

But this is not sufficient in and of itself. Jesus does more than draw us a perfect picture that shows us the way ahead. He takes care of all the rubble in the road, which is to say, the hindering sins that keep us from God's will for us. This is the role of the cross.

There have been many interpretations of just why Jesus' death on the cross is necessary for our salvation; and in some ways, Wesley uses them all. In some places Wesley talks of Jesus' death as a ransom; in others of his writings he talks of Jesus as our substitute, taking our punishment in our place. Jesus is also the "satisfaction" paid in order to satisfy God's offended honor. And sometimes Wesley uses the law court imagery of a prisoner standing in our place before the bar. Perhaps Wesley's most dominant image is that we owe a debt to God that we cannot pay. So Jesus pays it for us.

That debt must be interpreted in light of what Wesley says is God's creative intent for us, and in light of Jesus' fulfilling of that intent. But our failure has introduced the radical suffering in the world of destruction and death. So the cross is like the final gathering up and focusing of all this rubble, this damnable destruction, into one supreme act of death in which we are all symbolically present—just as we were symbolically present in Adam. If this were the end, of course, nothing would have been accomplished, save one more miserable death. But resurrection becomes God's ultimate answer to death. Christ bursts through the bonds of death, declaring life and its flourishing as the final answer of God to our sin.

And so Wesley says that we now are called to live by the law of faith. By faith we identify with Christ's life, and so his life becomes a blueprint for our own. By faith we identify with Christ's death, dying ourselves to those sins that would block us from living from, in, and toward the love of God. The forgiveness of sins means freedom from the shackles of sin, moving from death toward life. By faith we identify with Christ's resurrection, and are ourselves born into the new life of fulfilling God's will for us: developing all the powers with which we were created to the glory of God. This is the law of faith, but of course it is also the law of love. Hear Wesley on this point (page 62):

Q. 4. Is love the fulfilling of this law?

A. Certainly, it is. The whole law under which we now live is fulfilled by love. . . . Faith working or made active by love is all that God now requires of human beings. God has substituted not sincerity but love in the room of angelic perfection. . . . [Q. 5. A.] It [Love] is the aim of every commandment of God. It is the expected outcome of the whole and every part of the Christian life. The foundation is faith, purifying the heart. The aim is love, preserving a good conscience.

To be identified with Christ through faith is to be freed for the law of love. And this law, like the Mosaic law before it, is for the sake of guiding us toward the fulfillment of what we are each and communally called to be by God's creative intent.

The rubble is cleared, the path goes before us, and we can now get on with what God intended us to be.

Justification, Sanctification, Glorification

Wesley summarizes the law of faith in three words: *justification*, *sanctification*, and *glorification*. The words can be understood temporally, but Wesley meant more than that. That is, one can logically say that first we are justified, and therefore enabled to live a sanctified life, which naturally leads beyond our death to a state of glorification with God. But Wesley tended to see each of these terms as deeply interrelated, so that they all apply at all times throughout our Christian life.

For example, Christ's death (Wesley refers to it as "the atoning blood") was a multifaceted act with deep ramifications for the whole of how we live. It does not apply to one moment of our lives, as if it were summed up and dismissed with the notion that God objectively forgives us (a change in our condition relative to God) so that we might subjectively begin a new life (a change in our real circumstances in our daily lives). Rather, this forgiving, rubble-clearing nature of God covers us throughout our whole lives; we are never without it, nor should we ever wish to be.

It is likewise with sanctification. Sanctification is precisely the loving of God with our whole heart, and our neighbor as ourselves; it is the fulfillment of all the intent of God. With the rubble cleared away, we are to live fully toward love. As we will see later, this can be described both as instantaneous event and as process. While we live it daily, it is what God has intended for humanity long before we ourselves entered this race, and it shall be the fulfillment of humanity throughout eternity. Sanctification spans all times.

Glorification, also, cannot be restricted to a single time, as if it were a distant goal to be achieved when we finally die. How could this be the case? If our living from, in, and toward God's love is in fact the glory of God, then glorification is something we are about throughout our Christian lives. And insofar as God is in Christ, and we are identified with Christ, then we, too, participate in God's glory through Christ. What was it with those shepherds on the hillside of Judaea? "And the glory of the Lord shone around them," and the angels sang, "Glory to God in the highest heaven" (Luke 2:9, 14). God's glory is not distant, but present in the knowledge of God through Christ both in Bethlehem and here in our own places. It is ever so.

So, then, this is the framework within which Wesley's doctrine of Christian perfection takes place. It is set within the creative will of God, who creates us with an intent toward our flourishing. Our flourishing is not an automatic affair, as if we ourselves had nothing to do with it. To the contrary, our flourishing is accomplished only insofar as we, in conjunction with our communities, develop all the powers with which we were created, to the glory of God. We participate with God in creating the flourishing of ourselves and all others in this earthly community.

We seem to be uncommonly good at messing up our end of this situation, but that is not enough to stop God from fulfilling the divine intent. Jesus Christ becomes for us God's way of dealing with our recalcitrance and our sin, forgiving us in order that we shall be made able to get on with the task for which God called us into being in the first place. And that task is Christian perfection.

Chapter Two

Explanations and Exasperations

In the first half of *A Plain Account*, from its opening pages through the lengthy account of Jane Cooper that ends on page 59, Wesley describes how he has held to his understanding of Christian perfection throughout his life, and how the first annual conferences were devoted to discussions of Christian perfection. In the process, he recounts again and again the difficulties he had in conveying to people exactly what he meant by Christian perfection: what it was, what it was not, and why it was scriptural. No matter how clear he was, it seemed his words always got twisted to mean something that was not at all his intention, which is why he attempted this plain account of exactly what he believed Christian perfection to be. Christian perfection is love of God and neighbor, exercised by the grace of God through our continuous development of all the powers with which we were created, to the glory of God, which is the service of love. It seems quite clear and simple, but Wesley met continuous resistance in his preaching and teaching.

What Christian Perfection Is

Have you ever been in the situation of explaining something to someone over and over again, but the listener still misunderstands you? You wonder if both of you are using the same dictionary or if there is something inarticulate in the way you are expressing yourself. If you have ever been in this situation, you should have some sympathy for John Wesley as he tried repeatedly to explain exactly what he meant by Christian perfection. It is, as he says so often in this little book, a heart filled with love of God and neighbor. Hear him in the following typical passages:

- . . . both my brother and I affirmed to this day:
  (1) that Christian perfection is the love of God and our neighbor
      that leads to deliverance from all sin;
  (2) that this is received only by faith;
  (3) that it is given instantaneously, in one moment;
  (4) that we are to expect it, not at death, but every moment (pages
      39–40).

- Christian perfection is loving God with all our heart, mind, soul,
  and strength. This implies that no passions contrary to love remain
  in the soul. It means that all thoughts, words, and actions are governed by pure love (page 41).

- Perfection is nothing higher and nothing lower than this: the pure
  love of God and human beings. In other words, loving God with
  all our heart and soul, and our neighbor as ourselves. It is love

governing the heart and life, running through all our tempers, words, and actions (page 44).

- Scriptural perfection is pure love filling the heart and governing all the words and actions (page 48).

- It is loving the Lord our God with all our heart, mind, soul, and strength; and loving our neighbor, every human being, as ourselves, as our own souls (page 62).

That Pesky Word *Perfection*

Wesley is certainly quite clear in these statements of explanation. But part of his problem was that pesky word *perfection*. Our tradition has a long history of interpreting that word to mean something that is unchangeably complete in itself, needing nothing other than itself in order to exist, and never being any better (for that would challenge the perfection of the previous state) or worse (because if decline was possible, perfection had not been attained). Thus perfection meant a rather static state. Such an interpretation of perfection had much to do with the development of the Christian understanding of God as being impassive, immutable, totally impervious to change. This was quite unlike the dynamic description of God given throughout the Christian and Hebrew Scriptures. But the notion of God as perfect in the Greek sense of immutability shaped much of Christian history and theology.

The Greek notion of God's perfection also deeply affected the Christian understanding of the Bible. Whenever the Scriptures spoke of God changing in any way, such as in Jonah 3:10 ("God changed his mind about the calamity that he had said he would bring . . ."), these changes were considered to be only figures of speech that were not really intended to speak about how God really is. They were called anthropomorphisms and discounted. However, passages that spoke of the divine faithfulness as unchanging were seized upon to claim that nothing whatsoever could change within God. For example, Malachi 3:5 speaks of God's steadfast will toward justice: God is "against those who oppress the hired workers in their wages, the widow and the orphan, against those who thrust aside the alien." In this, says Malachi 3:6, "I the LORD do not change." But the theological utilization took the passage out of its context of God's unfailing will toward justice and turned it into support for the static perfection of God.

Thus, for Wesley to apply the phrase "Christian perfection" to our actual lives was to run counter to the usual understanding of the word. Almost by definition, *perfection* and *human* were contradictory terms. To be perfect meant there could be no change, neither for the better nor for the worse. In fact, perfection was so contrary to the human condition that most people thought perfection was something that could apply to humans only after death, when God would finally make the Christian perfect. To speak of "growth in perfection," as Wesley did, was against the common sense of his time.

What Wesley meant by *perfection*, as is clear from the passages quoted earlier, was love for God, neighbor, and self. Should he have dropped the troublesome word *perfection* and stayed with the more acceptable word *love*? It certainly would have made things easier for him (and us!); but in a sense, *love* is just as ambiguous a word as *perfection*. The problem if Wesley had used *love* is that everyone would have thought they knew just what Wesley meant without bothering to ask him to define *love*, for doesn't everyone know what love means? We who live more than two hundred years after Wesley can be thankful that he used the offensive word *perfection*, since it forced him repeatedly to clarify what he did and did not mean by it. In the process, of course, he forces us to reconsider our own understanding of divine perfection. If the Greek understanding distorts the meaning of the Scriptures and is so totally contrary to our experience, perhaps the Greek word no more applies to God than it does to us. But we shall return to this later.

What Christian Perfection Is Not

Meanwhile, we must probe more of Wesley's explanations in the first half of the book, where he deals not only with what perfection is, but with what it is not.

Christian perfection is not freedom from ignorance and mistakes. Turn to page 18, paragraph number 12 (1), and see how Wesley stresses this point. Because the things we know are so conditioned by our particular perspective, our bodily and spiritual senses, and our limitations of context, there is no way that we can be "perfect in knowledge." Therefore, we are neither infallible nor omniscient. We are, as Wesley says more than once, liable to error.

There are radical implications to these plain statements. At first they seem simply to be true. Of course we are not infallible! Of course we are not omniscient! Who would deny this? But Wesley takes these uncontroversial judgments and pushes them to their conclusions. If we are subject to error, and if we are not free from ignorance and mistakes, then some of the things that we think must be erroneous. Which things are these? The conundrum is simply this: If we could name where it is that we are making errors in judgment, then we would immediately change our opinions so that we might be correct. After all, who does not wish to be correct? But by definition we simply cannot know where it is that we are making errors in judgment. We are fallible in our knowledge.

If we took this seriously, would it not change our attitudes and actions toward those who disagree with us? Would it not push us away from defensive arguments and turn us instead toward exciting dialogues? For perhaps the one who thinks differently is right. And if we truly desire to identify our incorrect judgments, then surely we should not spend all of our time trying to convince others that we are right. Instead, we would be most curious about those who thought we were wrong. Perhaps we could learn from them, and so come to more sound opinions and judgments. And of course if we worshiped and worked within a community of like-minded people who were also going on to perfection, then their attitude toward opinions different from their own that we might hold would likewise be eager and curious rather than belligerent and defensive. Can you imagine living in such a community? What a difference such attitudes would make to the serious differences of opinion that arise in any group setting. Recognizing that Christian perfection is not being right in everything we think we know would provide opportunities to exercise the love that Christian perfection is when controversies arise in the church.

Predestination Versus the Universal Grace of God

We will have more to say about these insights when we discuss Wesley's first advice to those seeking Christian perfection in our next chapter. But here we must point to another writing in which Wesley carries out this theme, his sermon on "A Catholic Spirit." One of the most heated theological controversies in Wesley's day had to do with the Calvinist position on predestination. According to Calvin, God controls all things, and therefore controls who will and who will not be saved. Free will is a gift that follows from Christian faith; there is no free will prior to Christian faith. Therefore, persons are not free to respond to God until God gives them the response of faith. There is no cooperative human response until by grace faith is given. Therefore, God controls who does and does not respond to the gospel.

Wesley was adamantly opposed to this position, for he believed in the universal grace of God. God is so fully gracious that all people, not just some people, are touched by the grace of God. Whether or not one responds to God's grace depends upon the person's free response. Hence the call to believe the gospel appeals to a real freedom. Obviously, then, Wesley thought the Calvinists wrong in their opinions concerning predestination, for both positions could not be right.

Church Worship

In addition to this vexing difference of theological opinion, there were also many differences in terms of church worship. The Anglican church had a formal liturgy, whereas some of the worship services at Methodist chapels were essentially preaching services. Was there only one correct way to worship God?

Wesley's sermon "A Catholic Spirit" advocates an openness to those who differ from ourselves on such things. Instead of asking for theological conformity—which would be impossible, given our fallibility—he asks for friendship. "Is your heart as my heart? Then give me your hand!" he asks, quoting Joab from the sermon text 2 Kings 10:15. This is a plain application of the implication of our fallibility of knowledge; it pushes us toward openness toward the other.

Christian Perfection in Practice

Openness and recognition of our proneness to error does not lead to a kind of Christian indifferentism, where it doesn't matter at all what one believes. This would be far from a Wesleyan position. Indeed, Wesley insisted upon a number of beliefs, Christian perfection being one of them. One searches the Scriptures, studies the tradition, applies one's reason, and probes one's own experience to determine which things are relatively unshakable within one's Christian faith. And these things are not done all by oneself but in the community of believers, where it is possible to share insights, discuss problems, learn from one another. In the context of the community we develop and refine our formulations of Christian faith. Openness to other opinions, and recognition of our fallibility, does not become an excuse to believe nothing or anything. Rather, it becomes the occasion to apply oneself seriously to thinking about Christian faith, and to listening to those who think otherwise in order to see what we might learn. And when differences seem to be irreconcilable, one nonetheless offers friendship and fellowship to the other. This is Christian perfection in practice.

Wesley also says that Christian perfection does not save us from ordinary human frailties. He names these frailties as slowness of understanding, inarticulate pronunciation, shortcomings, and temptations (page 18, and reaffirmed on page 41). Once again, naming these frailties as compatible with Christian perfection has enormous implications for the body of believers called Methodists. It means that we do not divide ourselves according to IQ ratings, valuing the "thinkologists" among us more than others. To the contrary, we should expect that there are varieties of gifts within each congregation, with quickness of understanding being but one of the gifts.

With regard to "inarticulate pronunciation," we may consider this a quaint peculiarity in our own day—until we remember that Wesley was writing in a context where how one spoke revealed one's class. The language of the upper classes was far different from the language of the lower classes; and indeed, our situation in America is not really so dissimilar. It is not just that we have regional accents that reveal our geographic origins. In a society continually in flux through constant immigration patterns, our speech often reveals whether English is our first language or not, or whether we have been to college, or to what degree we have integrated into mainstream society. "Inarticulate pronunciation" was not an indicator of class just in Wesley's society; it is the same indicator in our own society. And Wesley assures us that Christian perfection has nothing to do with our finely drawn value distinctions concerning class or origin. To the contrary, Christian perfection is possible across the whole social spectrum. A migrant in the fields may or may not have the fullness of Christian perfection; a highly educated and economically successful person may or may not have the fullness of Christian perfection. Whether they do or not depends upon their responsiveness to the profligate grace of God. So Wesley cautions us not to make quick judgments concerning one's standing in grace that are drawn according to a hierarchy of social values. God's values streak across our values, judging them according to how they measure up to the lavish grace of God.

And Christian perfection does not protect one from temptation. Why should it? Temptation belongs to the human condition; we are always struggling in the balancing act between our own needs and desires and the needs and desires of the whole. Christian perfection does not mean the struggle is over, only that victory is ever possible, no matter what the struggle. The love of God, poured into our hearts, leads us always in the direction of that which is the larger good, that which leads to wholeness and wholesomeness. But it is not an automatic thing, as if we were suddenly turned into autonomons with no choices to make. How could love be compatible with such nonsense? Rather, through Christian perfection we build up a character that tends toward the good. The same temptations that would lead us away from the good become the power to strengthen continuous choices toward the good. Exercising choice toward the good in the presence of alternatives is precisely what the daily building up of Christian character is all about.

Ah, but what if we not only have temptations but yield to temptations? What then? Surely this is the great contradiction of Christian perfection. But Wesley would not have it so. He would remind us that "if we confess our sins, he who is faithful and just will forgive us our sins and cleanse us from all unrighteousness" (page 20; 1 John 1:9). Yielding to temptations could cause us all kinds of difficulties, but it could never cut off the continuously offered grace of God. Difficulties were entailed not as God's punishing us for yielding, as if God were some stern taskmaster threatening us with a stick should we depart from a given code. To the contrary, the trouble with the sins to which temptation might lead us is that the sins by definition are attitudes and/or actions that contradict love; they lead to the breaking down of the good, whether of ourselves or of the community. Thus yielding to temptation naturally creates problems, building up resistances within ourselves or others to the love of God. But God is so profligate in love, so unceasingly invested in our being restored to the divine image, that God continuously gives grace enabling us to come back to love. When we are faithless, God is yet faithful, calling us to respond to grace. Yielding to temptation is a setback, but it need not be the end of the story.

Recognizing Christian Perfection

Well, then, Wesley's interlocutors wanted to know, if Christian perfection does not protect you from all these things—ignorance, temptation, frailty, and even mistakes—how would you possibly recognize a person who was perfect? Wesley found such questions exasperating. He was dealing with the notion that perfection somehow implied an ethereal creature for whom nothing ever went wrong. But in our concrete human situation, many things can indeed go wrong. What perfection calls for is the fullest development of our powers within whatever frail situation we find ourselves. This development might indeed be what Wesley called "hedged . . . in by outward circumstances" (page 47). For example, a person might be afflicted with some debilitating disease that causes frequent or even constant pain. Can this person know Christian perfection? The answer, of course, is a resounding yes. He or she can develop powers to whatever degree is possible and use these powers in service to the love of God and neighbor. The fullness of the image of God might not be quite so dramatically apparent as in one who enjoys vibrant health. But here Wesley employs the tale of the widow's mite to suggest that the one who is "hedged in" might actually be living a fuller degree of Christian perfection than is the other.

Part of Wesley's point is that the question of who does and who does not enjoy Christian perfection is not for us to judge, for we have no basis for judging others truly (see, for instance, pages 50 and 51). We do not know the other's full circumstances, for the hedges with which the other must deal are not necessarily visible to our eyes. The one person whose circumstances we do know is ourself. Rather than spending our time worrying about other people's state of Christian perfection, we would be far better occupied questioning our own souls.

Pursuing Christian Perfection

And how, precisely, are we to do that? Wesley is quick to answer the question on page 49. Here it is quite evident that we are in fact Methodists: there is a method for pursuing the goal of Christian perfection! We are to be vigorous and zealous in keeping the commandments (which are, you will recall, channels through which love can flow throughout society). We are to deal with whatever our own hedges are; we are to fast, to pray, and to attend on all the ordinances of God. These ordinances are, of course, worship and the sacraments.

It might seem, from this list, that the method Wesley advocated was nothing but sheer discipline, sort of like gritting our teeth and getting on with all these necessary items. But to view it that way is completely wrong, for it fails to see the reason for the method, which is nothing but the grace and love of God. For Wesley, each of the abovementioned methods is a means of grace. By caring about the commandments, engaging in spiritual disciplines, and actively attending on the ordinances, we open ourselves to the wonderful grace of God that flows through these channels directly into our souls. It is sort of like going to a light switch in order to illumine a dark room. The electricity is always there, but we have to move the switch in order to let the current flow to the lamp that in turn gives light to the room. Each of these disciplines is like a light switch, connecting with the constant energy of God. God's energy is God's love, pouring into us in order that we ourselves might become loving creatures. So the method of obedience, spiritual discipline, and attendance at worship is not some kind of a "works sanctification"; instead it is a means of opening ourselves to the empowering grace of God whereby we might become loving people.

The Effects of Christian Perfection

And what would we be like, then, as loving Christians? Wesley deals with this on pages 45–46, and also in the long account of Jane Cooper on pages 56–59. First, he suggests that Christian perfection has the effect of causing a soul to pray constantly, to rejoice always, and to give thanks without ceasing. This is a recurring theme throughout the book; it is a way of saying that the soul's fundamental fulcrum point is God, no matter what forms of activity may be going on. That is, Christian perfection is a sort of soul-orientation, a deep resting in the security of God's love. It is deeper than an emotional reality; it is instead a kind of stance toward life that underlies everything one does. Because of this continuous assumption of God's presence and God's love, there is a depth of gladness and gratitude in the soul—rejoicing and thankfulness. And since God is the resting point within, there is an openness toward communion, a kind of prayerfulness that characterizes life. That is, the triadic refrain of prayer, rejoicing, and giving thanks refers to the wellspring within one's soul, the God-orientation of one's being. It is not that one goes around with prayer beads in a constant murmur of verbal prayer, nor that one continuously waves hands wildly to indicate religious joy, nor that one laughs happily and says thank you in the face of tragedy. These are surface acts. The praying, rejoicing, and gratitude of Christian perfection define the depths of a soul connected to God. Outward actions are then responsible and responsive to whatever the circumstances might be, whether tears of compassion or pain, or patience, or even fierce struggle toward conditions of well-being for those who suffer.

Notice the extended passage on page 16 where Wesley spells out such thoughts.

> A Methodist constantly presents his or her soul and "body as a living sacrifice, holy, acceptable to God." Without reserve Methodists completely devote themselves, all they have and are, to the glory of God. Every power and strength of the Methodist's soul, every part of his or her body, and all of his or her talents are constantly employed according to the Master's will.

Restored to the Image of God

Does it seem like a tall order? It would be, were it not for the key phrase just prior to these sentences, "Love is the source of this obedience." The meaning is twofold. In the first place, it is God's love that is the empowering source of our full development of every power and strength of our soul and body. And in the second place, precisely because of God's empowering love, our own love grows so that we can develop all our powers to the glory of God. It is from love and for love that we become who we can be in order to offer our best selves in love to God and others.

Wesley calls this state being restored to the image of God. Notice just how many times Wesley uses the phrase "image of God." You can find it on pages 23, 25, 33, 48, and 49, as well as on many pages in the later portions of the book. In order to understand the importance of this phrase, remember Wesley's understanding of salvation as given in Chapter One. God created human beings in order that they should develop all their powers to the glory of God, which is to say, toward loving God and neighbor. To be so created was to be created in God's own image, for God's full being is, in Wesley's words, "boundless love." God's aim in creation, says Wesley, is to create creatures who will be the image of God's own love, first because they are made from God's love, and second because they are made for God's love. Sin is that which is against love; it is uncreation, and as such it is most definitely not the image of God. In Christ we receive the forgiveness of sins, not as an end in itself, but as a means to the end of the restored image of God. With our sins forgiven, they no longer block God's creative intent toward our being in the image of God. Therefore, in Christ we are once again empowered to develop all our powers as much as possible within our circumstances for the sake of becoming fully loving creatures. Thus Wesley's constant reference to the image of God simply flows from his understanding that God's creative intent for us now flows freely. We are restored to the image of God, and this is Christian perfection.

This understanding shows why Wesley's critics were so far off the mark when they thought that perfection was possible only following death. If that were the case, then the redemption given to us through Jesus Christ would do us no earthly good. But how is it possible that so great a salvation should be without earthly effect? For Wesley this concept would be absurd. If Christ redeems us, then Christ takes away the curse of sin in all its blocking, uncreative wreckage. This, then, means that with sin cleared away, God's creative work can begin anew in us. God enables our response so that we can get on with the purpose of creation, which is the development of our creaturely powers toward the love of God and neighbor. God does not wait until some "sweet by and by" to call us to our created end; God moves toward it the moment that we respond in faith to God's prevenient grace, God's ever-given call to be open to the love of God. Wesley takes the word that NOW is the time of salvation with utmost seriousness. Christian perfection is for this life.

Christian Perfection: Wesley's Lifelong Conviction

Throughout this first section of *A Plain Account*, Wesley gives a history of his own life's conviction concerning Christian perfection, and also an account of the way that the annual conferences dealt with it. With regard to his own history, he picked it up in 1725, when he was 23 years old (page 11). While reading Jeremy Taylor's *Rule and Exercises of Holy Living and Dying*, Wesley was greatly taken with Taylor's words about purity of intention. A year later, these thoughts were reinforced through reading Thomas á Kempis's *The Imitation of Christ*, and again through William Law's writings. Through these writings, and certainly through his constant study of Scripture, he was convinced that Christians were called to walk as Christ walked. He preached on this in 1733 and throughout his time in Georgia. What is most interesting in this account of his continuous conviction that salvation relates here and now to this life is that although he continues his account through 1739, he never mentions the Aldersgate experience that we consider so essential to Methodism. Instead, the focus is entirely on his sustained conviction that what God intends, God can do. Through the restored image of God made available through Christ, we can be empowered to lead lives of love. We often think of Aldersgate as a conversion experience for Wesley, but in his own reflections on his life it is not the initial reliance on God that is central, but the effects of that reliance in the possibility of developing all our powers to the glory of God in love.

On page 33 Wesley begins talking about the conferences. He held the First Conference on June 25, 1744, with six clergy and all the lay preachers present. The topic of the conference was serious consideration of the "doctrine of sanctification, also known as perfection." The Second Conference was August 1, 1745, and again the main topic of conversation was Christian perfection. The Third Conference was on May 13, 1746, and the procedure was a careful review of the deliberations of the first two conferences. At the Fourth Conference on June 16, 1747, the topic was again the doctrine of perfection. There is no question that this significant doctrine was pivotal not only for John Wesley but for Methodism itself.

The Life of Jane Cooper

Wesley concludes this sustained argument that Christian perfection is the goal of Christian life by illustrating it in the life and death of Jane Cooper. The story begins on page 56 and continues through 59. The significance of the account is this. In contrast to the doubt that so many cast concerning the possibility of having a heart full of love in this life, Wesley gives a concrete example of such possibility. Furthermore, in contrast to the notion that Christian perfection would protect a person from all manner of dreadful things, Wesley chooses as his example a woman in the prime of life who has fallen prey to an illness that claims her life. She is, indeed, "hedged in by outward circumstances." But she is a witness to the fulfilled possibility of one whose full powers are developed to the glory of God in Christian love. And finally, in a world that so often placed men as the best examples of what we are called to be, Wesley gives a woman as the best example of what we are called to be.

Wesley draws his description of Jane Cooper from letters she wrote and from eyewitness accounts. In a letter written in May, 1761, she tells of her agony of soul as she sought salvation and of the peace and joy that came to her in the experience of God's saving presence. But in November she became ill, seriously so; for within a few weeks she died. However, "prayer without ceasing, rejoicing, and in everything giving thanks" marked her life in her dying even as it had in her living. She became a witness to the power of God proclaimed in the closing verses of Romans 8, for neither pain nor death could separate her from the love of God in Christ Jesus.

With this account Wesley closes this section of *A Plain Account of Christian Perfection*, going on in the next section with the theological ground of the doctrine that we covered in our first chapter. The richness of Wesley's thought cannot be captured simply by organizing and summarizing his thinking; it must be encountered by a close reading of the actual text. But Christian perfection is not a doctrine to be studied and read. It is a Christian blessing to be embraced and lived. It is God's gracious call to become what we were created to be: creatures of God, developing all the powers with which we were created toward the glory of God. And the glory of God is the love of God, flowing everlastingly from God to creation, and—when mirrored in creation as the image of God—flowing back to God and through God to the whole realm of creaturely being.

Chapter Three
"Advices"

Happily, Wesley concludes his plain account of Christian perfection by giving advice to those who are so drawn to the doctrine that they yearn to open their lives to this love. In the earlier portions of the book, Wesley has clarified repeatedly what Christian perfection is not. Interestingly, his advices to those who yearn for Christian perfection take us into unexpected depths concerning how Wesley understood love.

Notice first of all on page 72 in the answer to Q. 31, that Wesley considers perfection to be an "ongoing work." No static doctrine here. And this ongoing work is the work of God "mixed with much human frailty." The assumption is that God works not *on* us, like taking a suit coat or dress off of a rack and putting it on us regardless of fit. Rather, God works *in* and *with* us, adapting God's work to our condition of frailty. And should we be so surprised by this? Do we not, after all, say with pious wonder that God came to us in a manger? We have so glorified the Christmas story that we make crèches of gold or finely carved wood, forgetting the reality that mangers are really unattractive and smelly. But God came to us precisely in that unattractiveness; God comes to us in the midst of our frailty. God is like that, working with us as we are to bring us to what we can be. Christian perfection is an organic happening, a growing of the soul.

To those who yearn for Christian perfection, or worry lest they lose some portion of perfection, Wesley gives seven advices.

The First Advice: Beware of Pride

The first, not surprisingly, is against pride (Q. 32, page 73). We are to beware of pride and pray constantly against it; it is that besetting sin that so easily and invidiously takes hold of us. Or, to put it in a more active case, it is that sin that we so easily embrace.

Initially, one could nod quite comfortably in agreement with Wesley. Haven't we been told throughout our tradition that pride is like a Number One Sin? Isn't pride thinking more highly of ourselves than we ought to think? Isn't pride putting ourselves first and everyone else last? Pride is being "puffed up," so full of self that there is no room for God. Why, pride is the initial sin in that ancient Garden that got us all wrong in the first place. Surely such pride is a great danger to Christian perfection, for it would turn love all 'round wrong, focusing it on ourselves instead of God and others, until it wasn't love at all.

While Wesley might not oppose such an interpretation of pride, his approach to describing pride is astonishing, for he does not at all go in the above direction. Rather, for Wesley, pride is to be unteachable. "If you think you are so knowledgeable of God as to no longer need human teaching, then pride is at the door."

"Aha," we might respond, "but here I am studying Wesley's own teaching, so clearly I have escaped this particular sin of pride." Wesley will not let us off the hook so easily. He immediately says to his contemporary readers, "Yes, you need to be taught, not only by Mr. Morgan, one another, Mr. Maxfield, or me, but by the weakest preacher in London, yes, by all people. For God sends to us those whom God chooses to send."

The remarkable thing about Wesley's point here is that he is telling his readers that they need to be taught by those who oppose Wesley's own teachings. Mr. Morgan and Mr. Maxfield, while at one time closely associated with the Methodist movement, had taken Wesley's theology in directions contrary to Wesley's own thinking. One might expect Wesley to caution Methodists to beware of the extremes taught by these men and to stay to good plain teaching, such as, for example, Mr. Wesley's sermons and tracts. It would be similar to a situation today where a person staunchly holding a position of biblical inerrancy earnestly told others that they need to be taught by those scholars working in the Jesus Seminar. And the opposite is also true: those who study contemporary biblical scholarship should also see what they can learn from those who hold literally to every word of Scripture. Clearly, we find such a recommendation distasteful, for we far prefer to read only those who think in ways that are congruent with our own positions.

Think of the person who is most theologically different from yourself, and apply Wesley's advice: You have much to learn from that person. Or consider the rancor with which we regard those who take opposing views from ours on the social views of our day: homosexuality, war and patriotism, death penalty, abortion, capitalism. Do we really want to say we have something to learn from those who are on the "wrong" side of these issues? Shouldn't we close our ears when they begin to speak, recognizing them as the fanatics they are? Can anything good come out of those "Nazareths"? Wesley's answer is that we must listen to those who oppose us in order to learn from them.

We may think that the teaching thus far is radical enough, but Wesley takes it one surprising step further: "To imagine that none can teach you but those who are themselves saved from sin is a very great and dangerous mistake" (page 73). Ordinarily, we consider all Christians to be saved from sin, for isn't salvation precisely this? Who, then, are those who are not saved from sin? To be "saved from sin" is a Christian category; other religious traditions understand the basic human problem differently. Buddhists, for example, would not consider themselves "saved from sin," because the category is foreign to the way they construct the world. For Buddhists, suffering is the basic problem, not sin. Can we say, then, that those who would flee pride must even be open to learning from those of other religious traditions? What awesome consequences for growth in love! Can you imagine the kind of relationships that would begin to pervade this world if every religious person, while rooted in their own faith, was open to learning from another? To learn from another is to begin to understand the other. Wesley's small phrase, if applied to interreligious dialogue, offers a breathtaking vision of a network of friendship spreading over the world. Love would displace animosity, distrust, hatred, and, in our wildest application of this teaching, would mean that never again could religious teaching be used as an excuse to kill those who think differently. Could there ever be such peace on earth?

Wesley's interpretation of pride as being unwilling to learn from others is immensely important; it is the direct result of what Wesley means by Christian love filling the heart and mind. Remember that in the early portions of *A Plain Account* Wesley has taken some pains to point out that Christian perfection does not mean that we make no mistakes in thought and action. To the contrary, "It is as natural for a human being to mistake as to breathe" (page 61), and "because we live in fallible human bodies, we will be subject to errors in judgment and action. For neither love nor the 'anointing of the Holy One' makes us infallible. Therefore, because we are subject to faulty thinking and understanding, we cannot avoid error in many things" (page 63). Pride pretends to self-sufficiency, particularly in knowledge; and self-sufficiency turns the self into a sort of island, inhabited only by those who mirror in some sense one's own notions. How is this compatible with love? Love reaches beyond the self; love is open to the other; love dares to cross boundaries that would divide us. Therefore, the pride of thinking all of our own ways of thinking and acting are correct while those who oppose us are totally wrong is a great hindrance to Christian perfection, which is love filling all the heart and soul.

Before leaving this advice, one further caution needs to be raised concerning pride interpreted as unteachableness. To be unteachable is to think that our own way of thinking is God's way of thinking. It risks putting ourselves in the place of God, assigning the infallibility and omniscience that belongs only to God to ourselves. This is blatant idolatry. There is, then, a critically important function to disagreements. They can preserve us from idolatry. Disagreements show us that there are ways of thinking other than our own that we must take seriously, seeking to learn from them given the fact that we are fallible. And the other also can learn from us. So the great theological debates within the church should be taken as opportunities rather than crises. They may be God-given times for countering our tendencies toward the idolatry of thinking that Christian perfection is perfect knowledge instead of perfect love. For in the letter to the Philippians, that "mind which was in Christ" was not some encyclopedic knowledge, but the depths of unbounded love. And therefore the first advice for those seeking Christian love is the advice against thinking we have nothing to learn from those whose views oppose our own.

The Second Advice: Beware of Enthusiasm

And what is the second advice? Wesley gives it on pages 74–76, telling us to "beware of that child of pride, enthusiasm." This advice is strange to twenty-first century Christians, for whom enthusiasm is considered a good thing. We value enthusiasm as the antithesis of that lukewarmness defining the church at Laodicea in Revelation 3:15. To be enthusiastic, for us, is to care passionately for the gospel, and surely this is good.

But this was not how enthusiasm was defined in Wesley's eighteenth-century England. At that time enthusiasm was supposing that one had a special infusion of God's wisdom, apart from any earthly modes of knowing. It often involved speaking like a seer of things that were to come, something like present day "enthusiasts" who tell us with some satisfaction that as soon as all the Jews of the world crowd into Israel, nuclear weapons will explode in warfare between Israel and the Arab world, creating Armageddon and thus bringing about the return of Christ and the end of the world. Likewise, eighteenth-century enthusiasts saw themselves as having privileged knowledge from God that enabled them to predict earthly events. Enthusiasm, then, was the daughter of pride.

Enthusiasm, Wesley tells us, is also "expecting the end without the means," such as "expecting knowledge without searching the Scriptures and consulting the children of God, expecting spiritual strength without constant prayer and steady watchfulness, expecting any blessing without hearing the word of God at every opportunity" (page 74). Enthusiasm ignores the means of grace and the humbleness of ordinary Christian love, looking instead for extraordinary manifestations of "gifts of a new kind" (page 75) that it takes to be higher modes of spirituality. In the process, of course, the enthusiast then creates by definition a two-tier structure of Christianity, or what some have called a "holier than thou" complex.

I once experienced this myself, years ago, long before I'd encountered John Wesley's writings. I belonged at the time to a small community church. It was way back in the sixties, when charismatic renewal was sweeping many churches. The pastor of our little church journeyed to a place where people were laying hands on each other, and receiving the gift of tongues. This gift was taken to represent a higher plane of Christianity; and our pastor, thus enthused, came back to our little congregation inviting people to the laying on of hands and the gift of speaking in tongues. It seems strange now, looking back on it, but there were a number of us who were zealous for going on to this new form of spirituality, experiencing the gifts of the Spirit akin to the days of the apostles. And so I confess that I was one of those who received the laying on of hands and began using this glossolalia in prayer.

In some respects, it seemed a helpful gift; for so often we do not have the words to express our love to God in prayer, and it seemed that this strange new gift released one from the need for words. It was like pouring out one's soul to God in ways that seemed deeper than words could bear. And God, after all, hears us long before our speech, hearing our hearts as our voices. So this speaking in tongues seemed to cut out the muddle of language.

But then I began to notice the effect that this mode of worship was having on the congregation as a whole. Some of the Christians whom I respected most deeply, whose lives showed forth kindness and love in so many ways, just weren't comfortable with these new and unusual ways of worship. And it became apparent that they were feeling that somehow they must be second-class Christians, when it was obvious from their whole lives that they were models of Christian love. This new enthusiasm was creating discord in what had been a unified community. I think I was a heart Methodist long before I became acquainted with Methodism, for it seemed to me that love—that which makes for building up the community—was the criterion of the work of the Spirit. Since these enthusiasms were causing harm in the community, how could they be of God? While they might have value, as seemed apparent in prayer, was not a greater value being lost? And since God always hears the heart anyway, was this glossolalia business necessary? Maybe it was more like a minor convenience sort of thing that would best be dropped for the sake of the wider good, which was the community as a whole, where each was called to care for the other's well-being. The speaking in tongues phenomenon, at least of that particular time, was what Wesley would have called enthusiasm, something that got in the way of love. And so the little church quietly went back to loving God and one another without depending on strange utterances that produced division.

Wesley gives a test for determining that which is merely enthusiasm on page 74, and it includes elements of what Albert Outler eventually came to call the quadrilateral, that fourfold method of developing theology through Scripture, tradition, reason, and experience. Wesley says we are not to "hastily attribute things to God. . . . They may be from God. They may be from nature." We are to test things by the Word—but not in a proof-texting sort of way, citing a verse of Scripture as if it answered the whole question, as we could so easily have done in that little church had we simply stayed with the inclusion of speaking in tongues as a spiritual gift, subordinate to love, as recounted in 1 Corinthians 13–14. Instead we are to study the Scriptures, trying to understand to the best of our ability the context. Today we understand the complexity of context; it is like a spiral, beginning with the peculiarities of the surrounding texts and the structure of the writing, but extending to the cultural and historical context in which the text was written as well. In other words, we are to use all the powers available to us to understand the meaning of a text. This is far from proof texting. And we must use reason, knowledge, and human learning; for, as Wesley says, "Every one of these is an excellent gift of God and may serve the noblest purposes" (page 74). There is a certain irony in his saying this, for of course the enthusiast considers his or her "special" abilities to be extraordinary gifts from God. Wesley points to the ordinariness of everyday things as excellent gifts, always pointing to the greatest gift, which is, finally, simply love, filling the heart and guiding our actions.

Notice that when Wesley describes some things that enthusiasts have mistakenly identified as gifts of a new kind, page 75, he starts with items on which there is common agreement. Enthusiasts—and all Methodists—are enjoined to follow the first six steps for growing in grace: loving God with all our mind, soul, and strength, and seeking oneness with God and Christ. Like the injunction in Colossians 3:3, we are to have our life hid with God in Christ. But then see how the enthusiasts take these things away from the focus on love and turn them to special revelations and to a freedom from the works of love (number 13) and from human frailty (number 14). Christian perfection doesn't use love as the first steps that then take us beyond the works of love or the frailty of our human condition. Rather, love is the purpose of all our steps, it is the fullness of all we could ever hope for; it is the glory of God and the gift of God in Christ. There is nothing higher to which we should aim. "All visions, revelations, manifestations, whatever," says Wesley, "are small things compared to love" (pages 75). So the enthusiast's mistake is to take love not as the goal but merely as a baby-step means to an end that is not necessarily connected to love at all. This is topsy-turvy, for it is ordinary Christian love to God and neighbor that is extraordinary; love is the beginning, the middle, and the end; there is nothing higher. Beware of enthusiasm.

The Third Advice: Beware of Antinomianism

The third advice (pages 76–77) warns us against thinking that love cancels out the law of works. Such thinking is antinomianism, thinking that because we are called to love, works of the law are now null and void. Against this, Wesley points out that Christ "has adopted every point of the moral law and grafted it into the law of love" (page 76). Remember that the Mosaic law was intended to create a society whose laws channeled well-being to all, including the least, who were often litanized as the widow, the orphan, and the stranger (see, for example, Deuteronomy 14:28-29). It is true that the law, as the apostle Paul points out, condemns us by showing us how heartless we can be insofar as we need laws to insure that well-being prevails. Clearly, it would be better if we all cared so much that laws were no longer necessary. But this is not so; thus we need laws for at least two reasons. First, society's laws have as their deepest purpose the guarding of well-being for those who are least. Obviously there are corruptions of the law; too often the law is used to guarantee only the well-being of those who already have well-being. Wesley worked unceasingly for the well-being of the poor, addressing the laws in his own day that worked their ill-being, such as land enclosures that took away public grazing lands and debtors' prisons that punished the poor. And second, on the personal level, love constrains us to do all the good we can to all the people we can. The law of works is not nullified by love but fulfilled by love.

Notice Wesley's application of this advice on page 76. He begs us not to confine our good works or generosity only to Methodists, "much less to that very small part of them who seem to be renewed in love, or to those who believe yours and their testimony." He tells us not to make this our shibboleth. The word *shibboleth* is quite interesting, as the marginal notes in this edition of *A Plain Account* explain. If you turn to the passage from Judges 12, you will see just what a shibboleth theology is like. Two of the Israelite tribes were warring, and the Gileadites emerged victorious. To be victorious was often to slay those who were the foes—isn't that the way of the victor? The problem, of course, is that they were all Israelites, so there was no particular distinguishing feature whereby the Gileadites could recognize the Ephraimites, the losers. There was, however, a small difference of dialect, for the little word *shibboleth* was pronounced with a "sh" at the beginning by the Gileadites, and with a straight "s" sound at the beginning by the Ephraimites. The Gileadites had captured the fords, so when anyone attempted to cross the ford, they were forced to say "shibboleth." If they could pronounce it with the "sh" they were allowed across; otherwise, they were slain. And the text tells us that 42,000 met this fate. The interesting thing for us today is that the text doesn't give us any sense at all of what the word meant. It didn't matter what it meant, only that it was pronounced correctly.

Don't we do that sometimes in judging one another's faith? We set up certain dogmas, declaring that in order to be a right Christian you must believe them—for example, the virgin birth or original sin. But oddly enough, we do not require that people understand how the doctrines developed or what they might have meant in their original formulations, only that they "believe" them. And if they don't, they are clearly not the right kind of Christians. We no longer take off their heads, but there are other ways of putting people down when we have a shibboleth theology.

For Wesley, the shibboleth was restricting love and the works that flow from love only to those who are most like ourselves in terms of doctrine and lifestyle. "Do not make this your shibboleth!" (page 76). Far from despising either works or the means of grace, we are to be a people generous toward all.

Antinomianism, then, or thinking that there is no longer any use for law, works radically against love. Therefore, those who desire to grow in Christian love should be zealous for those works that express Christian love, whether socially through enacting laws that channel love, or personally—and congregationally— through good works that flow from depths of caring for the well-being of all.

One further consequence of antinomianism was to despise the ordinances of God as means of grace. Just as the antinomian spirit considered itself above the commands to express love in good works, the antinomian also considered himself or herself to be so blessed of God as to be beyond the need for any of the ordinary means of grace, such as study or worship services or disciplines of prayer or taking Holy Communion. To the antinomian, these things are helps for those who have not yet achieved true freedom from the law. The antinomian, then, valued freedom more than love, using freedom as a form of self-indulgence that obviated any need for discipline or good works. But Wesley's response continues to insist that the humility of love is the goal of Christian existence; there is no higher way. And the ordinances of God—whether spiritual disciplines, worship, or the sacraments— are means to opening us still further to the influences of God upon us in every moment. And the end to which God's influence is directed is that we shall become more deeply loving people. Therefore, we must not despise the means of grace but in a sense flee to them in gratitude for these methods by which we might become ever more attuned to the love of God for us, flowing through us, inspiring our own love to others.

The Fourth Advice: Beware of Sins of Omission

The fourth and fifth advices follow naturally after the cautions against antinomianism. The fourth advice warns us to beware of sins of omission. It is fairly simple to understand what Wesley means by sins of omission, particularly given his advice concerning antinomianism; for antinomianism most surely falls into the danger of sins of omission. In contrast, Wesley tells us that if we desire Christian perfection, we are not to neglect any opportunity for doing good of any kind (page 77). To me one of the most compelling illustrations of this teaching is Wesley's own life. I am profoundly moved by a passage from his journal recounting how, during a bitterly cold January, he fretted that the poor needed not only coal and bread but clothing as well; but the Society did not have enough money for the clothing. So Wesley went out into the streets of London for four days, begging for funds to buy clothes for the poor. "It was hard work, as most of the streets were filled with melting snow, which often lay ankle deep; so that my feet were steeped in snow-water nearly from morning till evening." His efforts yielded two hundred pounds! The date of this journal entry is January 4, 1785: John Wesley was 81 years old. "Do not neglect any opportunity for doing good" indeed.

The Fifth Advice: Beware of Desiring Anything But God

Wesley's advice concerning desiring nothing but God might seem a bit unusual, given his strong commitment to love of neighbor. For Wesley, though, love of God could never be separated from love of neighbor; the two commandments were two sides of one coin. Perhaps Psalm 37:4 clarifies the point, for the psalmist tells us that we are to delight ourselves in the Lord, and the Lord will give us the desires of our heart. The implication, of course, is that if indeed we delight in the Lord, the desires of our heart will change into conformity with God's own desires and God's unbounded love. Contrary to this, there is still the peculiar notion abroad that connects holiness with material wealth: "Delight yourself in God," such foolishness might say, "and you will get that red convertible, or great riches, or . . ." This kind of thinking is to delight not in God, but in mammon. As if to underscore such a point, Wesley includes these stringent words under this advice: "Allow no desire of pleasing food or any other pleasure of sense. Allow no desire of pleasing the eye or the imagination by anything grand, or new, or beautiful. Allow no desire of money, praise, or esteem. Do not desire happiness in any creature" (page 77).

Taken on their own, these words suggest a strong asceticism—and there is an element of asceticism in Wesley. But the full *A Plain Account* tempers these words. For example, in this passage we are not to desire "pleasing food," but on page 46 we are told that we might prefer pleasing to unpleasing food as a way of increasing our thankfulness to God, and that pleasures can increase our delight in God. Is Wesley saying two contradictory things, then? I think not. Rather, his point is that the dominating focus of one's life is to be the love from and toward God, and all other things have their place in relation to this focal point. Thus, "do not desire happiness in any creature" is not a contradiction to Wesley's lifelong care to alleviate the desperation and deprivations of poverty. He cared enough that people should be protected from the cold that he braved the sleet-filled streets himself; he fostered cottage industries that would provide means of sustenance for those whose lives had become impoverished by changing social structures; he took great care about people's nutrition and health. Surely the happiness of those he helped was not irrelevant. And surely he was not so impervious to what makes for happiness to think that warmth instead of cold could not be a cause of cheer. But he knew in the depths of his being that the fount of all joy—may we call it happiness?—comes from the grace and love of the sustaining God. Happiness is not the goal but the byproduct of the chief goal, which is openness to the grace and love of God.

To desire God is to delight in God, and to delight in God is to delight in that which delights God, which is the well-being of all creation. If God so loved the world that God gave Jesus Christ, then should we not also love the world toward its highest well-being? And doesn't that highest well-being entail love, a mutuality of love whereby all creation is interconnected in a mighty caring for one another's good, to the glory of God? Thus "you simply aim at pleasing God, whether by doing or suffering" (page 78), and all lesser goals fall into their rightful place.

The Sixth Advice: Beware of Schism

We come now to the sixth advice, which stands on a par with the first concerning pride and unteachableness, only now in an even stronger application to the community than is obvious in the first advice alone. That is, in the first advice it is not too difficult to read the advice purely in terms of the individual. While it does indeed apply to every individual, its import is toward the community, and this becomes apparent in the sixth advice. "Beware of schism," says Wesley, "or causing separation within the church of Christ. Such internal division begins when sisters and brothers in Christ, the members of his body, no longer have love 'for one another'"(page 78). Obviously, this advice relates to what happens when we ignore the first advice, which is to recognize our fallibility and to engage in learning from one another, whether the other agrees with us or not. This is reinforced by "Do not tolerate any thought of separating from your brothers and sisters, whether their opinions agree with yours or not. Do not dream that anyone sins because he or she doesn't believe you or take your word, or that this or that opinion is essential to the work, and both must stand or fall together" (page 78). What could be stronger? The plain sense is that theological differences of opinion are to be expected, not discouraged, in the community of faith. The unanimity to be sought is the unanimity of caring, respect, and love within the community.

Often we take disagreements in the church, particularly those where feelings run deep and the gulf between positions is seemingly unbridgeable, as signs of great sin. We think that one side is clearly right, the other side is clearly wrong, and the best way to deal with the issue is to get rid of the other side by conversion or rejection, and so to establish the "pure" church where everyone agrees on important issues. But when we are tempted in these directions, we have lost sight of the wisdom of Wesley. Deeply held disagreements become the occasion to exercise love by openness to learning from one another. In the process, we are protected from the idolatry of supposing that "our" side—whichever one that may be—is infallibly right.

Remember that these advices are precisely to Methodists, both individually and as a whole, to lead them toward Christian perfection, Christian love. This is the end toward which each advice works. We need to interpret Wesley's strong caution against schism in terms of the unlove that schism represents. To argue that it is absolutely necessary to split the body of Christ because of what appears to be irresolvable disagreement is to assume that one party is infallibly correct in whatever the issue is. But this is idolatry, taking one's own thinking as equivalent to the infallible judgment of God. First, such idolatry absolutely refuses to learn from those who differ from a given opinion. It is, therefore, a despising of the other, a refusal of love. It is unlove. Second, such a split assumes that intellectual or ethical agreement is more important than love. Like the enthusiasts, it subordinates love to something else, in this case, to right opinion. In doing so, far from seeking communion with the other, it seeks separation; but this is to stop the possibility of living in one community/congregation/denomination in love. It is unlove.

Against this, Wesley instructs us to "expect contradiction and opposition, together with crosses of various kinds" (page 79). Rather than viewing these contrary views and people as a sad misfortune in the church, Wesley says we should be thankful, seeing their presence as from God and, therefore, as "useful and necessary to you" (page 79). Think of this in relation to growth in love. Loving only those with whom we agree is like trying to build up muscle strength by exercising with a feather. But loving those with whom we disagree is exercising with the hard stuff; it demands pushing our ability to love to places it has not yet reached, and we grow in Christian perfection. Thus we are to view disagreements as opportunities to exercise love.

The love that we exercise is deeper than mere emotional warmth, although it certainly can include such warmth. Love respects the intentions of the other, whether one feels warmth toward the other or not; love cares beyond one's emotions toward the well-being of the other; love seeks to break beyond all boundaries in concern for the other. Love does not require that the other be simply a mirror of oneself; love delights in the otherness of the other and seeks relation, learning, mutual caring. Love creates dialogue, assuming that the other also respects oneself or one's own party, and that the other also seeks learning and mutual caring. This is essential not only for the person who seeks to grow in love but for the community as well. Schism cuts all of these possibilities away, like some guillotine severing a head from its body. Schism denies the possibility of love and therefore lessens the body of Christ by denying the possibility of Christian perfection. Schism is like a cancer on the body, creating disease and ill-being. Wesley cautions us to shun it like the plague it is.

Strong disagreement can hurt one's own sense of self; it challenges the rightness of one's own position and, therefore, can feel like an undercutting of one's personal integrity. The defensive response is often anger toward the other and a lashing out in righteous indignation. But Wesley cautions us not to be "thin-skinned, irritable, or combative," and we are to receive contradictions and oppositions "with humility, meekness, gentleness, and sweetness" (page 79). By recognizing our own fallibility, and the great importance of the body of Christ, we can grow beyond our defensiveness and reach toward a genuine care for the other.

Schism, then, is a terrible witness that the body of Christ has failed in its love. In times past, such failures have indeed been accompanied by bloodshed and hatred in the name of correct belief. The bloodshed and hatred are but the consequences of pride and self-righteousness that ultimately lead to schism. Hence Wesley's strongest words to those seeking Christian perfection are to guard against all temptation to divide Christ's body so wantonly, and to seek instead to use the occasion of disagreement and disapproval as opportunities to reach new heights of learning how to love.

The Seventh Advice: Be Exemplary in All Things

After these six advices designed to help us toward Christian perfection, toward being a people whose hearts and minds are filled with the love of God governing all our thoughts and actions, what advice could possibly be left? Why, just one! Wesley finally advises us to "be exemplary in all things" (page 80). He tells us in this short-est advice of all that we should be careful in our dress, in little things, in the use of money. And we should look to the usefulness of our lives in this world, for the one who loves loses no opportunity to care for the well-being of those who are loved. Since God's love is boundless, we who seek to be filled with the love of God put no boundaries on our own love. It is no wonder that one of the goals of Methodism is "to spread scriptural holiness over these lands" ("Our Theological Task," *The Book of Discipline of The United Methodist Church*), for scriptural holiness is nothing other than Christian perfection, and Christian perfection is nothing other than love. As a Methodist people, given to growth in the love of God, we shall, as Wesley says, be "a light shining in a dark place," daily growing in grace, until "entry into the eternal kingdom of our Lord and Savior Jesus Christ will be richly provided" for us. So may we be.

Chapter Four

Sparks From the Fire

Have you ever sat around a campfire on a summer evening, watching sparks take off from the flames like fireflies flitting into the softly beckoning night? While the fire keeps burning, these little spinoffs delight us with their randomness, till they disappear into the enveloping darkness. Something like this happens at the end of *A Plain Account*. The fiery focus on Christian perfection continues to the end: Wesley not only summarizes his whole teaching on pages 86–87 (paragraph number 26), but, unable yet to leave it, he concludes with an even briefer summary on page 91 ("Brief Thoughts on Christian Perfection"). Make no mistake, the subject is Christian perfection. But suddenly toward the end of this book, little sparks begin to fly off, reaching for the starry heights. These sparks are rather astonishing teachings on prayer, tossed off almost as an afterthought as Wesley summarizes Christian perfection.

It's not as if Wesley saves all mention of prayer until these closing pages. To the contrary, since he holds that prayer without ceasing is a part of Christian perfection, he has certainly referred to prayer at various points throughout the book. But here at the end he says rather unusual things about prayer. My thinking is that this is because the book recounts not only his teaching but the manner in which Christian perfection informed the way he lived his whole life through. The last entry in the book is dated 1767, when Wesley was 64 years old. He was a man of prayer, and one learns a thing or two through a lifetime of praying. So I strongly suspect that these strange sparks simply reflect his own continuously deepening experience. He was not intending to teach us a theology of prayer; to the contrary, he intended to teach us plainly about Christian perfection. His "sparks" about prayer spring from his own inner life. To learn from this great man is to let his experience enter our own. His sparks on prayer become invitations to us in our own praying, testing out what he says, seeing where it leads us.

So let us follow these sparks, put them together, and see what they tell us about Christian perfection.

Spark 1: Participating in God's Creative Power

The first spark, on page 81, follows the concluding advice concerning exemplary living. He says:

> Although all the graces of God depend on God's abundance, God is generally pleased to attach them to the prayers, the teaching, and the holiness of those whom God gives to be our examples in faith.

At first glance this sentence might slip right by us; we might not think it strange to say that God generally attaches grace to the prayers of others. And, of course, in this passage it is not only prayer but teaching and exemplary living that are means whereby the grace of God comes to us. Whereas traditionally the sacraments were considered the means of grace, Wesley broadens the understanding, seeing God as using every available means to mediate grace to us. God is gracious!

But push the thought about God's grace attached to prayer for a bit, for it suggests an awesome thing. God is full of grace, and grace is that active will toward our good, that generosity of love, that superabundance of sharing from the divine nature itself. In the deepest sense, grace depends not upon us, but upon God's own self. Grace describes God's nature. Well, then, why do our prayers enter into the availability of grace at all? We need to check out similar statements from Wesley to probe his meaning.

On page 83, in (5), Wesley says:

> God does nothing but in answer to prayer. Even the people who have been converted to God without praying for it themselves (which is extremely rare) were prayed for by others. Every new victory that a soul gains is the effect of a new prayer.

The context, of course, is conversion. Nonetheless, is it not remarkable for him to say that "God does nothing but in answer to prayer"? There is one more pertinent spark on this theme on page 85:

> God frequently conceals the part that we children have in the conversion of other souls. However, whenever a soul is converted to God, we may boldly say that one of the chief causes is the person who persistently intercedes before God for that conversion.

The force of all three of these passages from Wesley is that there is a kind of cooperation between us and God, a sort of responsiveness that becomes a vehicle of grace. The source of grace is God's own character, but the operation of grace seems to be tied in some way to the creature's response. Of course we could simply explain this away by noting that this is how Wesley talks about prevenient grace, but we must first notice that these sparks about prayer qualify our usual understanding of prevenient grace. Usually, this grace affirms the pervasive presence of God to all people. This presence in itself depends upon the omnipresence of God, the fact that there is nowhere that God is not. And since God is gracious, clearly God's presence anywhere is gracious as well. Prevenient grace is that "calling grace" that goes before us, enabling us to be responsive to God.

But Wesley is deepening that definition by connecting the release of grace to prayer. Indeed, by going so far as to say that "God does nothing but in answer to prayer," even in the context of conversion, he is indicating something radical about the creative power of God. How strange it is! Before we rush to call the statement a hyperbole, think about the wonder in saying that God does nothing except in answer to prayer. What if prayer isn't something that just emerges with human existence? What if prayer says something fundamental about God's creative power, even before God called human beings into existence?

Think about the possibilities. The earth is very old, and humans are relatively young. If dinosaurs lived for millions of years, we fragile little humans are merely thousands of years old—not very old at all in the larger scale of things. But did dinosaurs pray? What about before dinosaurs? Do plants pray? mud? rocks? What sense does it make to say that God does nothing except in answer to prayer when there are no humans to pray?

Play with the notion that all existence, not just the part that is rational, has some form of power to respond to God. After all, doesn't the book of Genesis talk about creation as a kind of calling and responding process long before humans are created? Genesis 1 suggests that God speaks a word, and in response to that word something comes into existence. God then judges that response ("and God saw that it was good") and calls again. Each call builds upon the previous response, so that an orderly creation emerges. And everything that is, is what it is in and through its responsiveness to the creative call of God.

Genesis speaks in terms of vast generalities: light, land, vegetation, animals, humans. But as we look at the creation around us, we know that each of these is multiple; and Genesis also would have it so. The ocean teems with different kinds of fish, the air is filled with birds, and vegetation is a flourishing mass of plants and trees. If we think about God's massive creation of so great a variety of things in light of Wesley's connection of grace and prayer, it suggests that God's call is not some distant thing, heard across vast expanses, but that God's call is always a near thing, closer to us than our jugular veins, as an old Rabbinic saying would have it. Creation, then, is an intimate thing between God and that which God is calling into being. The response is deeply important to what happens next, and insofar as responses are variable, so is creation. Creation itself is an act of grace that involves call and response in a kind of dance between God and that which is coming into being.

God Does Nothing But in Answer to Prayer

If you have followed me thus far, now is the time to look again at Wesley's statement, "God does nothing but in answer to prayer." Wouldn't it be so? God's creative power is exercised in awesome calls that are near, enabling, empowering. But the reason God creates in such a way is that a response is required. "Let there be . . ." calls for an answer, so that cells are created, are organized, and spring into various forms of existence in response to God. Is this not a rudimentary form of prayer? Maybe the creative dance between God and all creatures is the seed of what will become conscious communion with God, once God calls into existence creatures who can sustain this communion. How intimate, then, is creation! Once, we might have thought of God's creating power as a far-off act of transcendent might, but with Wesley we reconceptualize God's creativity as the wooing, immanent power of God that works with us. That brooding Spirit of God hovering over the face of the waters in Genesis is close, as close as prayer. When we pray, then, we are participating in God's creative power. What overflowing grace! Prayer, or responsiveness to God, is like a channel through which God's grace flows, so that between the call and the response something happens.

This thought is reinforced by Wesley's statement on page 83 about "the need we have of grace to sustain the life of God in the soul. This life God gives can no more survive one moment without God's grace than the body can without air." God's creative power did not stop at some moment in the long-ago past, as if creation were a once-upon-a-time sort of thing. Rather, the creative power of God's call and the creatures' responses that we see in Genesis is always operative. If it weren't, creation would cease. And this action of God is the basis of what we know as prayer. God calls; we respond. Prayer is a response to the ever-present calling grace of God.

It is not so strange to say such a thing. Wesley, after all, was no follower of Calvinistic notions of predestination; he did not think God arranged who would respond this way or that to the gospel call. To the contrary, Wesley was convinced that we are responsible for how we respond to the grace of God. God works *with* us, not *on* us. The different happenings of the world show how we have responded to the ever-given prevenient, creative, and empowering grace of God. The little statement "God does nothing but in answer to prayer" suggests that through prayer we have insight into the way God works not just with us but with all of creation. Applied to our own life then, particularly in the way we turn to God in conversion, Wesley's statements make eminent sense. Prayer opens us to God's calling, and insofar as we respond to those calls, channels are opened through which God's creative grace pours. When we pray, the creative grace of God pours through us to do what God can do now that we are open to the work of God.

Obviously this can affect our own lives, but it can also affect the lives of others. Prayers make a difference to what can happen to someone else. This is no magic thing; it is the way of God's working in the whole universe. Prayer is an opening to the grace of God so that things happen in the world that could not happen apart from prayer. God works through our responsiveness, our intentional opening of ourselves to the work of God so that we can be used of God in God's work in the world.

Does this mean we control what God can do? No, it simply means we make a difference to what God does. God working through prayer does not mean that everything we pray for is going to happen, because there is no way that we know all the circumstances about which we pray. Remember Wesley's comments about the "hedges" of outward circumstances that surround us, limiting our possibilities? We do not know what hedges might affect the outcome of our prayers. All we know is that prayer is going to make a difference. What that difference is, is up to God and what God is doing with the rest of the world. We who follow Wesley, then, must take prayer with utmost seriousness.

Spark 2: Bearing the Faults of Others and Our Own

Turn now to yet another spark. This one begins on page 82:

> We ought to quietly suffer whatever befalls us, to bear the faults of others and our own, to confess them to God in secret prayer or with groans that are too deep to be spoken in words. . . . We are to bear with those we cannot change and be content with offering them to God.

This teaching is rather alarming. To catch its full force, imagine that you know someone whom you consider to have a contentious spirit. This person manages to stir up trouble, instigating enmity between groups of people, all in the name of something righteous. In your opinion, you rather think this person is at fault, with a kind of self-righteousness that looks down on those in other camps. You certainly would not name this person as a model of Christian perfection. Perhaps it would not be too out of line to think that you somewhat despise this person; but whether you do or not, you sadly think that this person is certainly sinning in these destructive attitudes and actions.

Now go back to Wesley's teaching. We are to "bear the faults of others and our own, to confess them to God in secret prayer." The practical import of this statement is that when we judge someone to be acting wrongfully, we are to recognize our own faults as well and confess both to God in secret prayer. We are accustomed to the fact that we are to confess our own sins before God, but to confess the sin of the other as if it were our own? How can this be? But notice how practicing this leads to Christian love.

For one thing, if we confess the sins of the other as if they were our own, it means that we must reckon with our own tendencies toward the same sins we identify in the other. We are no stranger to those negative attitudes and actions we are confessing. Perhaps, by the grace of God, we have not actualized those sins; or perhaps, given circumstances, we do not have the same "hedges" around us that the other has. Perhaps we are less tempted toward these sins. But the capacity to sin in those ways is nonetheless within us. By confessing the sins as if they were our own, we begin to identify with the one for whom we pray.

But don't we say that our own salvation comes about in Christ's identification with us in our sin? If we identify with the other, is this not a Christlike activity? And just as Christ's identification with us springs from divine love, perhaps it is the case that our identification with the other can begin to mediate divine love toward that other. Our naming their sin—not in self-righteousness, but in solidarity despite the distastefulness of the sins we have identified—may be used by God toward the other's good. And it will certainly soften our own hearts toward the other. So we are to "bear with the other," content to offer her or him to God in our prayers.

If we follow Wesley in this teaching, there are wondrous implications for how we would be church together. We would not only be praying for others, but we would know that as others saw faults or sins in us, they would be faithfully lifting us to God, confessing our sins as their own, asking God's strengthening forgiveness for us. We would be bearing one another's burdens, and so fulfilling the law of Christ, as the apostle Paul writes about in Galatians 6:2. We would be recognizing our common humanity, our common struggles. We might grow in humility as well as in love. How caring our churches would be!

Spark 3: Praying Without Ceasing

But there are further sparks. In the concluding paragraphs of Paul's first letter to the Thessalonians, Paul writes "rejoice always, pray without ceasing, give thanks in all circumstances" (1 Thessalonians 5:16-18). Wesley often cites these characteristics as expressions of Christian perfection. On page 83 he expands on unceasing prayer.

> When we think of or speak to God, whether we act or suffer for God, all is prayer when we have no other goal than God's love and the desire to please God.
> All that a Christian does, even in eating and sleeping, is prayer when it is done in simplicity, according to the command of God, without either adding to or diminishing from it by personal choice.
> Prayer continues in the desire of the heart, though the understanding is worked out in outward actions.
> In souls filled with love, the desire to please God is a ceaseless prayer.
> . . . All God requires . . . is that . . . they continually offer to God the desires and promises that naturally flow from perfect love. These desires, being the genuine fruits of love, are the most perfect prayers that can flow from such love.

Wesley describes the whole of life as a kind of living prayer. This can happen because of the distinction he makes between "the desire of the heart" and "outward actions." That is, by no means does he suggest that in order to be a living prayer, one must stay on one's knees in a holy place for hours at a time. Rather, he is referring to a kind of basic resting in the presence of God that is at the same time an orientation of openness to God. This is the depth level of one's being, even as one goes about one's ordinary daily work.

Remember the discussion above about creation and the need for God's sustaining grace in every moment of our lives. Ask yourself how you experience this grace. If you simply think in terms of your consciousness, you might be chagrined to say that you do not really notice grace much except in special times. But Wesley says you live by the grace of God in every moment. God's grace is constantly infused into you at the depth levels of your being. You are so used to it that you do not notice it, much as you do not really notice the air you breathe unless suddenly it is taken away. God is always present to you.

The life of Christian perfection assumes this constancy of God's gracious presence. It becomes the fundamental lodestone of one's being, the *sine qua non* of one's life. God pervades life at its deepest levels, always present in the depths of all things, including each person.

The purpose of God's presence is gracious. Grace is God's empowering call to us toward that which is best in our particular circumstances. Since we can count on God's guidance toward the good, our conscious lives are not constantly probing our inward states of being. Rather, we trust God to be working within us, and therefore we are free to think and act about whatever occupies our days and our cares in this world. It is as if there is a deep resting place for our spirits, even while we are mightily engaged in some energetic work.

Because of this trust in the God who is present toward our good, when we experience anxiety—as we most assuredly will from time to time—our response is to take that fundamental trust in God into our conscious thinking and orient ourselves to God in prayer. It is possible for the peace of God to break through our anxieties so that we can deal with those anxieties as well as with the situations that provoke anxiety.

Prayer without ceasing, then, is a fundamental stance of trust in the living presence of God toward the good, no matter what our circumstances. It is an utmost dependence upon the grace of God, underlying all that we do or think. It releases us for the intensities of life, and for Wesley these intensities included countless hours on horseback, preaching, organizing, dealing with problems and issues of the societies, dealing with personal relationships, writing, reading, meeting with friends and colleagues, and of course the daily activities of meals and sleep. Who could think of a more industrious person than Wesley? Praying without ceasing does not cut into the things we have to do; it is a release and freedom for those things precisely because it is the underlying foundation of our whole lives. Or, as Wesley says on page 84, "Add to constant watchfulness and prayer steady employment." Praying without ceasing is a freeing thing, enabling our zest for fulfilling God's call in our lives.

Intentional Times of Prayer

But lest we think, "Because I pray always, I don't need a set time for private prayer," Wesley has a strong caution. This actually comes from his third advice against antinomianism on page 76. The antinomians, as you recall, felt they were above all law and beyond all disciplines, and Wesley rightly cautions us against antinomianism. He sees a rhythm between the fundamental trust in God that is unceasing prayer and the intentional times of bringing concerns, praise, thanksgiving, and intercessions before God. Each actually informs the other. Intentional times of prayer strengthen our underlying trust in God, and the underlying trust in God rises to expression in set times of prayer. Remember, prayer is not only an orientation; it is also a work that mediates grace to the world. Therefore, it is essential that we do that work, offering our prayers to God so that God may use them to further God's own purposes in the world. It is a sad and weakening mistake to assume that we pray without ceasing and therefore need no special times of prayer.

Set times of prayer are also important because, as Wesley says on page 84, "It is good to renew ourselves from time to time by thorough self-examination of the state of our soul as if we have never examined it before." The underlying trust in God must not be taken as an automatic purification of our lives; we can drift into a complacency that hinders our spiritual growth. We can easily drift into an acceptance of hurtful attitudes simply because we become accustomed to them. To counter this, prayer is necessary as an openness to God in self-examination, questioning ourselves in the presence of the One who cares most for our good. Unceasing prayer, then, must be supplemented by various kinds of intentional prayers.

Spark 4: Connecting Through Corporate Prayer

Wesley also strongly states that prayer must be corporate, and not simply personal. That is, if one were of a pietistic bent, one could easily think that the most important kind of praying is that done privately before God alone. But remember, we are part of the body of Christ; and God works with us not as if we were the sole individual in the entire world but as members of the body of Christ. Corporate prayers are absolutely essential to the life of faith. He talks about this on page 78:

> As one said, "That part of our community, the private weekly meetings for prayer, examination, and instruction, has been the greatest means of deepening and confirming every blessing that was received by the word preached and of spreading it to others who could not attend the public ministry. Without this religious connection and fellowship, the most ardent attempts by mere preaching have proved of no lasting use."

and also on page 84:

> We ought to be in the church as the saints are in heaven, and in the house as the holiest people are in the church, doing our work in the house as we pray in the church, worshiping God from the depths of the heart.

By "the private weekly meetings," he is referring to the small groups that were essential to the Wesleyan societies. Public worship was supplemented by the organization of small bands that met at a specified time for praying, talking about one's spiritual journey, and teaching. Prayer is not just private but must also be corporate, and corporate prayers foster spiritual growth for both the individuals and the society as a whole, and therefore for the society's influence and work in the world. Spiritual growth, of course, is always connectional; it relates us more deeply toward one another in love and binds us in loving actions toward those beyond our own circles.

Think about the corporate praying that usually takes place during a Sunday morning worship service. While the pastor is praying, he or she is doing so not as an individual but as the voice of the congregation lifted to God. The work of the congregation during that corporate prayer is to echo it in their own hearts, joining with the pastor and with one another as the unified body of Christ—whether in confession, intercession, thanksgiving, or simple praise. In the process, we are both individual and corporate at the same time.

Korean Christians have learned this lesson well. Often in Korean worship there is a time when all members of the congregation pray together individually, aloud, simultaneously. Each voices the concerns of his or her heart and the needs of the wider community. Because each is using his or her own words, the prayer is personal; but because all are doing this together at the same time, the prayers are deeply corporate. There is an attunement to one another in the praying, so that the voices rise and fall together, like a choir creating an anthem. One could hardly find a stronger illustration of the sense in which prayers are personal and corporate at the same time.

There is another implication in the fact that we are called to corporate prayer. We are together the body of Christ. It is not just that we are the body of Christ when we come together for Sunday worship; we are always the body of Christ. Thus when we pray in solitude, there is a sense in which we are only seemingly solitary, for we are still part of the body of Christ. Our personal praying has a corporate dimension, just as our corporate praying has a personal dimension. Because we are one body in Christ, the sharp lines we tend to draw between individuals and the church as a whole shift and blur; they are moving lines, manifest now in this way, now in that. Our prayers, offered in the name of Christ, unite us as one body. It is necessary and good, then, that the corporate dimension of our praying should come to expression where two or three or more are gathered together, our separate prayers joining as a single offering to God.

Spark 5: Offering Our Good Works as Prayer

Thus far we have been focusing on Wesley's words about prayer that refer to our common understanding of prayer: private prayer, corporate prayer, underlying prayer, confessional prayer, and prayer as a means of grace. But Wesley does not confine prayer to these traditional activities. He also thinks of the good works that we do as a kind of prayer.

> If we were not utterly impotent, our good works would be our own property. But now they belong entirely to God because they flow from God and from God's grace. While giving rise to our works and making them sanctified, God is honored in us through them.
>
> One of the cardinal rules of religion is to lose no opportunity to serve God. Because God cannot be seen, we are to serve God in our neighbor. God receives such service as if it were done to God in person, standing visibly before us.
>
> . . . Charity [good works] cannot be practiced correctly unless. . . [we] offer it to God in humble thanksgiving. (page 85)

All of this, of course, follows from life as unceasing prayer. If the foundation is prayer, then all that follows is itself a form of prayer. Works of love are forms of worship offered to God, who empowers the works in the first place through unceasing grace.

But doesn't Wesley carry this to awesome extremes in the passage quoted? We are quite comfortable with the fact that we offer our works to God as a form of worship. Usually we understand this to be done in personal prayer. That is, we do the work and then offer it to God. But in this text, the actual doing of the work is already worship. Look at that line: "God receives such service as if it were done to God in person, standing visibly before us." This concept is radical! It reminds us of the passage in Matthew 25 where Jesus says that inasmuch as we have done good to the least of these, we have done it to him. Wesley says that God stands before us in the person of our neighbor, and that as we serve the neighbor, we are in fact serving God. And God accepts this service as worship. What could be more holy than this?

If we consider this teaching in the light of Christian perfection, it is not at all strange. We are told that we are to develop all of our powers—mental, emotional, physical—to the glory of God, and the glory of God is the love of God. We are told that the work of salvation is the renewal of the image of God in us, and love is this image. The love of God extends to all; it is expressed as grace; it is boundless; it encompasses all of creation, including the person "standing visibly before us." The love of God in us energizes us to act in conformity with the love of God. But that is precisely to meet the needs of the ones God loves, and those are all creatures. Acting in love toward the other, then, is like completing the circuit of God's love. It is the renewed image of God in the creature, which means that it is God's love toward the other exercised through us. This is the highest of callings, the highest of gifts, the highest form of worship, and it is Christian perfection. In this perfection, we love and serve our neighbor; in doing so, we love and serve God.

As usual, Wesley sees the possible pitfall in all of this, which is that we might get so enamored of thus serving God that we take great pride in it. After all, isn't it our service to God? Wesley saw a certain danger to good works. Works can subvert us from love of God that drives the works in the first place. And this thought brings us to the final spark concerning prayer with which Wesley concludes the book, just prior to his summaries. It also reveals why "spark" is such an appropriate metaphor for prayer.

Wesley begins to deal with the problem in the last lines of 85, which we have already considered and which speak of offering our works to God in prayer. When we do this, Wesley says we

> unite ourselves to God, in whom the soul expands itself in prayer, with all the graces we have received and the good works we have done, to draw from God new strength against the bad effects these very works may produce in us if we do not make use of the antidotes God has ordained against these poisons.

When we offer our works to God as prayer in the very doing of the works, then the works never do belong to us. They belong to God, for they are given to God in the process of doing them. This is easy to illustrate. When we give a gift to someone we love, perhaps for a special occasion such as a birthday or Christmas, we do not consider that the gift is really ours. It is not ours at all, not like some loan we are making to the person, whom we then allow to use our gift even though it is really ours. Even in the purchasing or making of the gift, we think of it as belonging to the one for whom we intend it. And once it is actually given, it is wholly the other's; it is within his or her ownership. The same is so when we give the gift of our works to God. They do not belong to us any more than birthday presents given to another belong to us. Gifts belong to the one to whom they are given. Doing good works in the spirit of prayer and worship, then, means that the works are always God's. And since it doesn't make sense to pride ourselves on something that is not ours, there's no point in priding ourselves in works. They are not ours; they are God's.

In the passage quoted, Wesley speaks of the offering of our works to God as a uniting with God. See how he continues this theme under the image of fire on page 86:

Fire is the symbol of love. The love of God is the beginning and the end of all our good works. But truth surpasses symbol. The fire of divine love has this advantage over material fire: it can return to its source and raise with it all the good works that it produces. In so doing it prevents corruption by pride, vanity, or any evil mixture. This can be done only when these good works have their beginning and their end in God. This is done through deep gratitude that plunges the soul into God as into an abyss. All that it is and all the grace and works for which it is indebted to God must be returned to God. This is a gratitude through which the soul seems to empty itself of good works so that they may return to their source, like rivers seem willing to empty themselves when they pour themselves into the sea.

When we have received any blessing from God, we need to withdraw, if not into our prayer closets then into our hearts, and say, "I come, Lord, to restore to you what you have given."

These ending words of *A Plain Account of Christian Perfection* recall words given near the very beginning, on page 13:

> Let the spirit return to God that gave it, with all that it holds dear. God does not ask of us any sacrifices other than the living sacrifice of the heart. Let our hearts be constantly offered up to God through Christ in flames of holy love.

It is more than our works that are offered to God in loving worship; it is ourselves. And if prayer is an openness to God in communion, then prayer is an instance in time of that which is our everlasting destiny. We are like those flames ascending to God. We who are called to be living prayers to God are the sparks flying—no (the image changes from heights to depths), plunging—into God. We are not only the sparks flying, the flames soaring, but the rivers emptying themselves into the sea of God. Our lives lived in Christian perfection, ever growing to the fulfillment of all the powers with which God created us, are wholly prayers. We are renewed in love, energized for love, and all the time we are uniting with God in and through our union with one another. We are bound together in love in this river of life flowing into God. And this is Christian perfection.

> My prayer hath power with God; the grace
> unspeakable I now receive;
> through faith I see thee face to face,
> I see thee face to face, and live!
> In vain I have not wept and strove—
> thy nature, and thy name is Love.
>
> Charles Wesley
> *Come, O Thou Traveler Unknown*

> Jesus, thine all-victorious love
> Shed in my heart abroad!
> Then shall my feet no longer rove,
> Rooted and fixed in God.
>
> O that in me the sacred fire
> Might now begin to glow,
> Burn up the dross of base desire,
> And make the mountains flow!
>
> O that it now from heaven might fall,
> And all my sins consume!
> Come, Holy Ghost, for thee I call,
> Spirit of burning, come!
>
> Refining fire, go through my heart,
> Illuminate my soul;
> Scatter thy life through every part,
> And sanctify the whole.
>
> *Collection*, #351; stanzas 4, 7–9